150 Recipes series

150

STUDENT *recipes*

INSPIRED IDEAS FOR
EVERYDAY COOKING

75p

CONTENTS

INTRODUCTION

For those at college or university and living away from home, or for others simply living on a restricted budget, this inspirational cookbook will fast become your friend in the kitchen. It will provide a great go-to source for delicious and creative budget recipes to suit all tastes.

So if you're feeling worn out and weary from studying, you need some brain-boosting food after a weekend wipe-out, you're taking time out to relax with mates, or you've just got the midnight munchies, we've got it all covered in this amazing selection of savoury and sweet eats and treats. With this fabulous range of simple, no-fuss meals you'll soon become a hotshot in the kitchen, creating truly scrumptious dishes for you and your housemates without making a big dent in your wallet.

We kick things off with a tempting selection of brilliant breakfast and brunch dishes, providing nourishing wake-up dishes to get those brain cells in gear for the studying that lies ahead. For a quick and easy start to the day, choose from superb staples like Cranberry Granola or Apple & Spice Porridge, or for something more substantial, pick Eggs Florentine, Breakfast Burrito or Sausage Frittata. If breakfast isn't your thing or you need something on the run, try smoothies like Muesli Motivator or Mango Magic Start-up.

To boost your brain power partway through the day and fuel your body to get you through to dinner time, our budget-busting lunches and snacks chapter includes a moreish medley of delicious eats from wraps, pittas and pâtés, to subs, sandwiches, salads and soups. Pick from temptations like Mighty Meatball Subs, Super-sized Fish Finger Sandwiches, Smoked Mackerel Pâté or Bang Bang Chicken Salad.

It's hard to beat mum's cooking, so if you're missing your folks and fancy something comforting, the next section features homely dishes (doubling as excellent exam fodder) like Quick Beef Stew, Sloppy Joes, Chicken Pie and Macaroni Cheese. For those who prefer dishes that pack a flavour punch, opt for Chilli con Carne, Cajun Chicken, Tandoori Salmon or Chilli Bean Stew.

Next up is a feast of flavourful dishes ideal for replacing expensive takeaways – so if you're tired out by the weekend these are the perfect pick-me-ups. Muster up your housemates and tempt them to the table with this savvy selection of munchies, including Monster Hot Dogs, Cheesy Chips and Sweet & Sour Pork. Or set senses ablaze with Colossal Lamb Kebabs with Hot Chilli Sauce, Vegetable Korma or Thai Green Chicken Curry.

Finally, satisfy sweet cravings with our sensational selection of desserts and puds. Enjoy feel-good favourites like Chocolate Pudding, Jam Roly-poly or Treacle Tart, or scrumptious chilled desserts such as Beeramisu, Eton Mess and Big Banana Split. Then, when you have some downtime to chill out with friends, wow them with creative cocktails such as Margarita, Club Mojito and Tequila Slammer, all great for sharing.

Thrifty Tips

- Become a savvy shopper. Get together with your housemates and all pitch in. Plan your meals ahead, write a shopping list and stick to it.
- Buy fruit and veg in season and pick up bargains from your local market.
- Cheaper meat cuts are great for budget cooking and ideal for casseroles and stews – perfect for feeding a crowd! Bacon bits and cold cooked meat or smoked salmon trimmings are great value.
- Own-brand supermarket products are often just as good as branded products, and much cheaper too.
- Leftovers can be used creatively. Use leftover roast meat to add to soups, salads or pies; use leftover cooked veg for frittatas, soups and pasta bakes.
- If you have a freezer, frozen vegetables are economical and nutritious, so stock up. Freeze meals, like soups, stews and pasta sauces, in single portions to reheat quickly another day.
- Instead of buying canned beans, buy dried beans, soak and cook them yourself.

KICK-START YOUR BRAIN

MUESLI

Serves: 4 **Prep: 10–15 mins** **Cook: N/A**

Ingredients

- 115 g/4 oz jumbo oats
- 55 g/2 oz ready-to-eat dried apricots, diced
- 30 g/1 oz pecan nuts, roughly chopped
- 55 g/2 oz sultanas
- 40 g/1½ oz dried cranberries
- 15 g/½ oz pumpkin seeds
- 15 g/½ oz sunflower seeds
- 1 tbsp sesame seeds
- milk or natural yogurt, to serve

Method

1 Place the oats in a large mixing bowl. Stir in the apricots, pecan nuts, sultanas, cranberries and the seeds, mixing well to combine evenly.

2 Serve with milk or natural yogurt. Store any leftover muesli in an airtight container.

★ Variation

Stir a freshly grated apple or pear into the muesli just before serving to add extra sweetness, fibre and vitamins.

BIRCHER MUESLI

Serves: 4 **Prep: 15 mins, plus chilling** **Cook: N/A**

Ingredients

250 g/9 oz rolled oats

1 tbsp wheatgerm

200 ml/7 fl oz milk

2 tbsp honey, plus extra to serve (optional)

2 tbsp natural yogurt

1 apple, peeled, cored and grated

150 g/5½ oz chopped nuts, such as macadamia nuts, cashew nuts or hazelnuts

mixed berries and fruit purée, to serve (optional)

Method

1 The night before serving, mix together the oats, wheatgerm and milk in a bowl, cover with clingfilm and chill overnight.

2 To serve, stir the oat mixture, add the honey, yogurt and apple, and mix well.

3 Spoon into serving bowls and top with the nuts and berries, if using. Drizzle over a little more honey or some fruit purée, if wished.

CRANBERRY GRANOLA

Serves: 8

Prep: 10–15 mins, plus cooling

Cook: 30 mins

Ingredients

2 tbsp vegetable oil
125 ml/4 fl oz maple syrup
2 tbsp runny honey
1 tsp vanilla extract
280 g/10 oz rolled oats
2 tbsp sesame seeds
4 tbsp sunflower seeds
4 tbsp pumpkin seeds
150 g/5½ oz dried cranberries

Method

1. Preheat the oven to 150°C/300°F/Gas Mark 2. Thoroughly mix together all the ingredients in a large bowl.
2. Divide the mixture between two baking sheets and spread out evenly. Bake in the preheated oven for 15 minutes.
3. Stir the mixture thoroughly, then put back in the oven and bake for a further 15 minutes. Allow the granola to cool completely on the baking sheets before serving. Store any leftover granola in an airtight container.

APPLE & SPICE PORRIDGE

Serves: 4 **Prep: 10 mins** **Cook: 15 mins**

Ingredients

600 ml/1 pint milk or water
1 tsp salt
115 g/4 oz rolled oats
2 large apples
½ tsp ground mixed spice
honey, to serve (optional)

Method

1 Put the milk in a saucepan and bring to the boil. Add the salt and sprinkle in the oats, stirring constantly.

2 Reduce the heat to low and leave the oats to simmer for 10 minutes, stirring occasionally.

3 Meanwhile, halve, core and grate the apples. When the porridge is creamy and much of the liquid has evaporated, stir in the grated apple and mixed spice. Spoon into bowls and drizzle with the honey, if using.

BERRY YOGURT CRUNCH

Serves: 4 **Prep: 15 mins, plus standing** **Cook: 5 mins**

Ingredients

75 g/2¾ oz rice, buckwheat or millet flakes, or a mixture

4 tbsp honey

500 g/1 lb 2 oz thick natural yogurt

finely grated rind of 1 orange

225 g/8 oz frozen mixed berries, partially thawed, plus extra to decorate

Method

1 Heat a dry frying pan over a medium heat, add the flakes and toast, shaking the pan, for 1 minute. Add half the honey and stir to coat the flakes. Cook, stirring constantly, until the flakes turn golden brown and slightly crisp.

2 Put the yogurt into a bowl and stir in the remaining honey and the orange rind. Gently stir in the berries, reserving a few to decorate. Leave for 10–15 minutes for the berries to release their juices, then stir again to give a swirl of colour.

3 To serve, spoon a layer of flakes into the bottom of four glasses, then top with a layer of the berry yogurt. Sprinkle with another layer of flakes and add another layer of the yogurt. Decorate with the reserved berries and serve.

MUESLI PANCAKES WITH HONEY

Serves: 4

Prep: 15 mins, plus standing

Cook: 10–15 mins

Ingredients

150 g/5½ oz plain flour
1½ tsp baking powder
pinch of salt
250 ml/9 fl oz milk
1 large egg
2 tbsp sunflower oil, plus extra for greasing
2 tbsp low-fat natural yogurt
140 g/5 oz muesli
honey, to serve

Method

1 Sift the flour, baking powder and salt into a bowl. Add the milk, egg, oil and yogurt and whisk to a smooth batter. Stir in the muesli and leave to stand for 5 minutes.

2 Lightly grease a frying pan and heat over a medium heat. Spoon tablespoons of batter into the pan and cook until bubbles appear on the surface.

3 Turn over with a palette knife and cook the other side until golden brown. Repeat this process using the remaining batter, while keeping the cooked pancakes warm.

4 Drizzle the pancakes with honey and serve immediately.

APPLE & CINNAMON PANCAKES

Serves: 4

Prep: 20 mins, plus standing

Cook: 20–25 mins

Ingredients

Pancakes

150 g/5½ oz plain flour
1 tsp ground cinnamon, plus extra for dusting
pinch of salt
250 ml/9 fl oz milk
100 ml/3½ fl oz apple juice
1 large egg
2 tbsp melted butter, plus extra butter for frying

Filling

apples, peeled and sliced
juice of ½ lemon
2 tbsp golden caster sugar

Method

1 For the pancakes, sift the flour, cinnamon and salt into a bowl. Add the milk, apple juice, egg and butter and whisk to a smooth, bubbly batter. Leave to stand for 15 minutes.

2 For the filling, place the apples, lemon juice and sugar in a saucepan over a medium heat. Cover and heat, stirring occasionally, until tender. Keep warm.

3 Put a small amount of the butter in a 20-cm/8-inch frying pan over a medium heat. Pour in enough batter to just cover the pan, swirling to cover in a thin, even layer. Cook until the underside is golden, then flip or turn with a palette knife and cook the other side until golden brown.

4 Repeat this process to use up all the batter. Interleave the cooked pancakes with kitchen paper and keep warm.

5 Spoon the apples onto the pancakes and fold over into fan shapes. Dust with cinnamon and serve immediately.

FRENCH TOAST

Serves: 6

Prep: 15 mins, plus standing

Cook: 15–20 mins

Ingredients

- 6 eggs
- 175 ml/6 fl oz milk
- ¼ tsp ground cinnamon
- pinch of salt
- 12 slices day-old white bread
- 55 g/2 oz butter or margarine, plus extra to serve
- ½ –1 tbsp sunflower oil or corn oil
- warm syrup, to serve

Method

1. Break the eggs into a large, shallow bowl and beat together with the milk, cinnamon and salt.
2. Add the bread slices and press them down so that they are covered on both sides with the egg mixture. Leave the bread to stand for 1–2 minutes to soak up the egg mixture, turning the slices over once.
3. Melt 25 g/1 oz of the butter with ½ tablespoon of the oil in a large frying pan. Add as many bread slices to the pan as will fit in a single layer and cook for 2–3 minutes, until golden brown.
4. Turn the bread slices over and cook on the other side until golden brown. Repeat this process with the remaining bread, adding extra butter and oil to the pan if necessary, while keeping the cooked French toast warm.
5. Serve the French toast in stacks with butter and warm syrup.

2
4

EGGS FLORENTINE

Serves: 2 **Prep: 15 mins** **Cook: 8–12 mins**

Ingredients

4 eggs

250 g/9 oz baby spinach leaves, chopped

4 tbsp single cream

2 wholemeal English muffins

salt and pepper

Method

1. Carefully break the eggs into a pan of simmering water and poach for 3–5 minutes, until the whites have set but the yolks are still runny.
2. Remove the eggs from the pan with a slotted spatula or spoon and put them on kitchen paper to drain thoroughly.
3. Meanwhile, place the spinach in a saucepan with just the water clinging to the leaves after washing and cook over a medium–high heat, stirring, for up to 3 minutes. Alternatively, place the leaves in a microwaveable bowl and heat on high in the microwave for 1 minute, or until wilted. Mix in the cream, a little salt and plenty of pepper.
4. Preheat the grill to medium. Slice the muffins in half horizontally before toasting under the preheated grill until lightly browned. Top each muffin half with a quarter of the spinach mixture and put an egg on top. Serve immediately, seasoned with a little extra pepper.

SALMON & CREAM CHEESE BAGELS

Serves: 2 **Prep: 15 mins** **Cook: 4–6 mins**

Ingredients

2 bagels
2 tomatoes, thinly sliced
grated rind of 1 lemon
1 spring onion, chopped
1 tbsp olive oil
125 g/4½ oz smoked salmon slices or trimmings
4 tbsp cream cheese
pepper

Method

1. Preheat the grill to medium–high. Slice the bagels in half horizontally and place them cut sides down on the rack in the grill pan. Toast under the preheated grill until lightly browned, then turn over.
2. Cover the bottom halves of the bagels with tomato slices. Sprinkle with lemon zest and spring onion, then season with pepper. Drizzle the olive oil over the tomatoes. Grill for 1–2 minutes, until the bagel lids are toasted and the tomatoes are lightly cooked. Remove the top halves and set aside.
3. Arrange the smoked salmon on top of the tomatoes and return to the grill for 1 minute to lightly cook the salmon and brown the edges in places.
4. Top each with 2 tablespoons of the cream cheese. Place the bagel lids on top and serve.

BACON BUTTIES WITH HOME-MADE TOMATO SAUCE

Serves: 2 **Prep: 20–25 mins** **Cook: 30 mins**

Ingredients

- 4 rashers smoked back bacon
- 30 g/1 oz butter, softened
- 4 slices thick white or brown bread
- pepper

Tomato sauce

- 2 tbsp olive oil
- 1 red onion, chopped
- 2 garlic cloves, chopped
- 250 g/9 oz plum tomatoes, chopped
- 250 g/9 oz canned chopped tomatoes
- ½ tsp ground ginger
- ½ tsp chilli powder
- 40 g/1½ oz dark brown sugar
- 100 ml/3½ fl oz red wine vinegar
- salt and pepper

Method

1. To make the tomato sauce, heat the oil in a large saucepan and add the onion, garlic and tomatoes. Add the ginger and chilli and season to taste with salt and pepper. Cook for 15 minutes, or until soft.
2. Pour the mixture into a food processor and blend well. Sieve thoroughly to remove all the seeds. Return the mixture to the pan and add the sugar and vinegar. Return to the boil and cook until it is the consistency of ketchup. Bottle quickly in airtight bottles or jars and store in the refrigerator until ready to serve.
3. Preheat the grill to high. Place the bacon under the preheated grill and cook, turning frequently, until the bacon is crisp and golden brown. Spread the butter over the slices of bread.
4. Place two rashers on each of two slices of bread, season with pepper to taste and spoon or pour the sauce over the bacon. Top with the other slices of bread and serve immediately.

1
2
3

RISE & SHINE SMOOTHIE

Serves: 1 **Prep: 15 mins** **Cook: N/A**

Ingredients

1 orange

55 g/2 oz cranberries

1 banana, peeled and roughly chopped

100 ml/3½ fl oz natural yogurt

Method

1. Peel the orange, then finely shred a little of the zest and reserve for decoration; discard the rest. Remove and discard the pips and most of the pith. Roughly chop the flesh and put it in a blender with the cranberries, then whizz.
2. Add the banana and yogurt and whizz again, until smooth.
3. Pour into a glass, sprinkle with the reserved orange zest and serve.

BERRY BREAKFAST SMOOTHIE

Serves: 1 **Prep: 10 mins** **Cook: N/A**

Ingredients

175 g/6 oz blueberries
115 g/4 oz cranberries
150 ml/5 fl oz natural yogurt
2 tsp honey
4 tbsp chilled water

Method

1 Put the blueberries and cranberries in a blender and whizz until smooth.

2 Add the yogurt, honey and water and whizz again.

3 Pour into a glass and serve.

MUESLI MOTIVATOR

Serves: 1 **Prep: 15 mins** **Cook: N/A**

Ingredients

20 g/¾ oz rolled oats

30 g/1 oz flaked almonds

½ ruby red grapefruit, peel and a little pith removed, deseeded and roughly chopped

150 g/5½ oz raspberries

juice of 2 oranges,

125 ml/4 fl oz chilled water

Method

1 Put the oats and almonds in a blender and whizz until finely ground.

2 Add the grapefruit, raspberries, orange juice and water and whizz until smooth.

3 Pour into a glass and serve.

MANGO MAGIC START-UP

Serves: 1 **Prep: 15 mins** **Cook: N/A**

Ingredients

½ pomegranate, seeds only

1 mango, peeled, stoned and roughly chopped

1 orange, peel and a little pith removed, deseeded and roughly chopped

Method

1 Reserve 1 tablespoon of the pomegranate seeds. Put the remainder in a blender and whizz until combined, then pour the juice into a glass.

2 Put the mango and orange in the blender and whizz until smooth.

3 Pour onto the pomegranate juice, sprinkle with the reserved pomegranate seeds and serve.

FULL ENGLISH BREAKFAST

Serves: 1 **Prep: 15 mins** **Cook: 20 mins**

Ingredients

2 pork sausages

2–3 rashers smoked back bacon

1 slice 2-day-old wholemeal bread

2 large tomatoes, halved

vegetable oil, plus extra for drizzling

2–3 mushrooms

1 egg

salt and pepper

Method

1 Preheat the grill to medium–high. Place the sausages under the preheated grill and cook for 12–15 minutes, turning occasionally, until cooked through and golden brown.

2 Meanwhile, place the bacon rashers in a dry frying pan and fry for 2–4 minutes on each side. Remove from the frying pan, leaving all the excess bacon fat in the pan, and keep the bacon warm.

3 Heat the frying pan over a medium heat and place the bread in the fat. Cook for 1–2 minutes on one side, then turn over and repeat.

4 Place the tomato halves under the hot grill. Drizzle with a little oil, season with salt and pepper to taste and grill for 3–4 minutes.

5 Add a little oil to a clean frying pan and fry the mushrooms. Remove from the pan and keep warm.

6 Add the egg to the pan and fry, basting occasionally, for 1 minute, or until cooked to your liking.

7 Transfer the sausages, bacon, fried bread, tomatoes, mushrooms and egg to a plate and serve immediately.

5
6

BOILED EGGS WITH SOLDIERS

Serves: 2 **Prep: 5 mins** **Cook: 8–10 mins**

Ingredients

4 large eggs
salt and pepper

Soldiers

4 slices crusty white bread, buttered and cut into thick fingers

Method

1 Bring a small pan of water to the boil – the water should be deep enough to cover the eggs.

2 Gently lower the eggs into the water using a long-handled spoon. Keep the water at a gentle simmer and cook for 3–4 minutes for a runny yolk and set white, or 4–5 minutes for a firmer egg.

3 Remove the eggs from the pan using a slotted spoon, drain quickly on kitchen paper and place in egg cups.

4 Season with salt and pepper to taste and serve immediately with the soldiers.

1
2
3

POTATO CAKES WITH BACON & MAPLE SYRUP

Serves: 4 **Prep: 20 mins** **Cook: 20–25 mins**

Ingredients

115 g/4 oz cold mashed potatoes

200 ml/7 fl oz milk

75 g/2¾ oz self-raising flour

pinch of salt

1 egg, beaten

sunflower oil, for frying

To serve

8 rashers back bacon

1½ tbsp maple syrup

Method

1 Put the mashed potatoes and milk into a food processor or blender and process to a thin purée.

2 Sift the flour and salt into a mixing bowl, make a well in the centre and add the beaten egg and potato purée. Using a balloon whisk, gradually mix the flour into the liquid ingredients, whisking well to make a smooth, creamy, fairly thick batter.

3 Heat a little oil in a large, non-stick frying pan. Pour a tablespoonful of batter per potato cake into the pan – you will probably fit about three in the pan at one time. Cook for 2 minutes on each side, until golden brown. Remove from the pan and keep warm while you cook the remaining potato cakes.

4 Meanwhile, preheat the grill to high. Place the bacon on a grill rack under the preheated grill and cook, turning frequently, until the bacon is crisp.

5 Divide the potato cakes between four plates, top each serving with two bacon rashers and drizzle with maple syrup.

SCRAMBLED EGGS WITH SMOKED SALMON & CHIVES

Serves: 2 **Prep: 15 mins** **Cook: 5–7 mins**

Ingredients

- 4 eggs
- 1 tbsp single cream or milk
- 55 g/2 oz butter
- 2 English muffins
- 125 g/4½ oz smoked salmon trimmings
- salt and pepper
- snipped fresh chives, to garnish

Method

1. In a bowl, whisk the eggs with the cream and salt and pepper to taste. Melt half of the butter in a small frying pan over a medium heat.
2. Add the beaten egg to the frying pan and cook for 1–2 minutes, stirring gently and pulling the mixture into the centre, as it begins to set. When the mixture is almost completely cooked, remove the pan from the heat.
3. Meanwhile, preheat the grill to medium. Slice the muffins in half horizontally before toasting under the preheated grill until lightly browned.
4. Spread the toasted muffins with the remaining butter and top with the scrambled eggs. Arrange the smoked salmon on top and garnish with the snipped chives. Serve immediately.

BREAKFAST BURRITO

Serves: 1 **Prep: 15–20 mins** **Cook: 8–10 mins**

Ingredients

- 2 egg whites
- pinch of salt
- ¼ tsp pepper
- 1 spring onion, thinly sliced
- ½ tsp vegetable oil
- 30 g/1 oz red or green pepper, deseeded and diced
- 2 tbsp canned black beans, drained and rinsed
- 1 wholemeal flour tortilla, warmed
- 15 g/½ oz crumbled feta cheese
- 2 tbsp salsa
- 1 tsp finely chopped fresh coriander, plus extra leaves to garnish

Method

1. In a small bowl, combine the egg whites, salt, pepper and spring onion and stir well.
2. Heat the oil in a non-stick frying pan over a medium–high heat. Add the red pepper and cook, stirring, for about 3 minutes, or until it begins to soften. Reduce the heat to medium, pour in the egg mixture and cook, stirring often, for a further 1–2 minutes, or until the egg sets.
3. Put the beans in a microwave-safe bowl and microwave on high for about 1 minute, or until heated through.
4. Spoon the cooked egg mixture onto the tortilla. Top with the beans, cheese, salsa and coriander. Serve immediately, garnished with whole coriander leaves.

1
2
4

SAUSAGE FRITTATA

Serves: 2 **Prep: 15–20 mins, plus cooling** **Cook: 20 mins**

Ingredients

4 pork sausages or vegetarian alternative

sunflower oil, for frying

4 boiled potatoes, cooled and diced

8 cherry tomatoes

4 eggs, beaten

salt and pepper

Method

1 Preheat the grill to medium–high. Arrange the sausages on a foil-lined grill pan and cook under the preheated grill, turning occasionally, for 12–15 minutes, or until cooked through and golden brown. Leave to cool slightly, then slice into bite-sized pieces.

2 Meanwhile, heat a little oil in a 25-cm/10-inch heavy-based frying pan with a heatproof handle over a medium heat. Add the potatoes and cook until golden brown and crisp all over, then add the tomatoes and cook for a further 2 minutes. Arrange the sausages in the pan so that there is an even distribution of potatoes, tomatoes and sausages.

3 Add a little more oil to the pan if it seems dry. Season the beaten eggs to taste and pour the mixture over the ingredients in the pan. Cook for 3 minutes, without stirring or disturbing the eggs. Place the pan under the preheated grill for 3 minutes, or until the top is just cooked. Cut into wedges to serve.

BREAKFAST OMELETTE

Serves: 1 **Prep: 15–20 mins** **Cook: 20–25 mins**

Ingredients

- 2 tsp sunflower oil
- 2 pork sausages
- 55 g/2 oz closed-cup mushrooms, sliced
- 2 rashers back bacon
- 2 large eggs
- 2 tbsp milk
- large knob of butter
- 1 tomato, cut into wedges
- pinch of dried thyme
- salt and pepper
- buttered toast, to serve

Method

1 Heat the oil in a frying pan and fry the sausages for 8–10 minutes, until golden brown and cooked through, turning frequently. Remove and set aside. Add the sliced mushrooms to the pan and fry over a high heat until golden brown. Set aside with the sausages.

2 Preheat the grill to high. Cook the bacon under the preheated grill, turning frequently, until the bacon is crisp.

3 Meanwhile, whisk together the eggs and milk in a jug and season to taste with salt and pepper. Wipe the frying pan clean and add the butter. Pour in the egg mixture and cook for 1–2 minutes, until the egg is beginning to set. Using a fork, draw the cooked egg into the centre of the pan to allow the runny egg to run to the edges. Remove the pan from the heat when omelette is almost set.

4 Thickly slice the sausages. Place the sausages, bacon, mushrooms and tomato on one side of the omelette. Sprinkle with the thyme and pop under the hot grill for 1–2 minutes, until sizzling. Slide the omelette onto a warmed plate, folding half of the omelette over the filling. Serve immediately with buttered toast.

1
3
4

SARDINES ON TOAST

Serves: 4 **Prep: 25 mins** **Cook: 8 mins**

Ingredients

4 fresh sardines (about 85 g/3 oz each), gutted, cleaned and heads removed

4 tbsp olive oil

4 slices crusty bread

1 garlic clove, halved

200 g/7 oz on-the-vine cherry tomatoes, cut into bunches

40 g/1½ oz watercress

25 g/1 oz fresh flat-leaf parsley

1 tbsp balsamic vinegar

salt and pepper

Method

1 To butterfly the sardines, lay them cut-side down on a board and press down along the backbone of each fish with your thumbs to loosen the bone. Turn each fish over and gently pull away the backbone. Cut the bone off at the tail end.

2 Preheat the grill to medium. Season the sardines with salt and pepper and drizzle with a little of the oil. Cook the sardines under the preheated grill for 3–4 minutes on each side, until cooked through.

3 Meanwhile, heat a ridged griddle pan until very hot. Rub the slices of bread with the cut garlic clove and brush with some of the remaining oil. Place on the hot pan with the tomatoes. Cook the bread for 2–3 minutes on each side, until lightly charred, and the tomatoes for 4–5 minutes, until just softened, turning frequently.

4 Place a cooked sardine on each chargrilled slice of bread. Mix together the watercress and parsley and pile on top of the sardines, then top with the tomatoes. Whisk the remaining oil with the balsamic vinegar and season to taste with salt and pepper. Drizzle the dressing over the sardines and serve immediately.

KEDGEREE WITH LENTILS

Serves: 4–6

Prep: 25 mins, plus standing

Cook: 55–60 mins

Ingredients

- 250 g/9 oz brown basmati rice
- 75 g/2¾ oz red lentils
- 1½ tbsp sunflower oil
- 1 large onion, finely sliced
- 1 tsp cumin seeds
- 1 tsp ground coriander
- pinch of asafoetida
- 825 ml/30 fl oz boiling water
- 1½ tsp salt
- 250 g/9 oz undyed smoked haddock
- 4 large hard-boiled eggs, chopped
- 2 large spring onions, finely chopped
- 2 tbsp chopped fresh parsley, to garnish

Method

1. Place the rice and lentils in a sieve and rinse under cold running water. Transfer to a bowl, cover with cold water and leave to stand for 30 minutes.
2. Meanwhile, heat the oil in a large saucepan. Add the onion and stir for 5 minutes, or until soft. Drain the rice and lentils.
3. Add the cumin seeds, ground coriander and asafoetida to the pan and cook, stirring, for 30 seconds. Tip in the rice and lentils and cook, stirring, for about 2 minutes, or until any excess liquid evaporates.
4. Pour over the boiling water and stir in the salt. Return to the boil. Stir, cover and reduce the heat to low, then leave to simmer for 40–45 minutes, or until the rice is tender and all the liquid has been absorbed.
5. Meanwhile, place the haddock in a frying pan and cover with water. Bring to just below boiling point, then reduce the heat to low, cover and leave to simmer for 10–15 minutes, or until the fish flakes easily. Drain the fish and remove all skin and bones. Flake the flesh into large chunks.
6. Stir the haddock, eggs and spring onions into the rice and lentils. Sprinkle with the parsley and serve.

BREAKFAST FLAPJACKS

Makes: 12 **Prep: 20 mins, plus cooling** **Cook: 25–30 mins**

Ingredients

- 250 g/9 oz butter
- 250 g/9 oz golden caster sugar
- 175 g/6 oz golden syrup
- 425 g/15 oz rolled oats
- 55 g/2 oz large raisins
- 55 g/2 oz ready-to-eat dried apricots, chopped
- 50 g/1¾ oz chopped walnuts
- 25 g/1 oz flaked almonds
- grated rind of 1 orange

Method

1. Preheat the oven to 180°C/350°F/Gas Mark 4. Line a 30 x 20-cm/12 x 8-inch baking tin with baking paper. Melt the butter, sugar and golden syrup in a large saucepan over a low heat, stirring until combined.
2. Remove the pan from the heat and stir in the oats, raisins, apricots, walnuts, almonds and orange rind. Stir well to combine. Spoon the mixture into the prepared tin and spread to the corners, flattening the mixture evenly.
3. Bake in the preheated oven for 20–25 minutes, or until golden on top. Leave to cool completely, before removing from the tin and cutting into 12 pieces with a sharp knife.

BLUEBERRY MUFFINS

Makes: 12 **Prep: 20 mins, plus cooling** **Cook: 25 mins**

Ingredients

280 g/10 oz plain flour
1 tbsp baking powder
pinch of salt
115 g/4 oz soft light brown sugar
150 g/5½ oz frozen blueberries
2 eggs
250 ml/9 fl oz milk
85 g/3 oz butter, melted and cooled
1 tsp vanilla extract
finely grated rind of 1 lemon

Method

1 Preheat the oven to 200°C/400°F/Gas Mark 6. Place 12 paper cases in a muffin tin. Sift togethe the flour, baking powder and salt into a large bowl. Stir in the sugar and blueberries.

2 Lightly beat the eggs in a large jug, then beat in the milk, melted butter, vanilla extract and lemon rind. Make a well in the centre of the dry ingredients and pour in the beaten liquid ingredients. Stir gently until just combined; do no over-mix.

3 Divide the mixture evenly between the paper cases. Bake in the preheated oven for about 20 minutes, or until well risen, golden brown and firm to the touch.

4 Leave the muffins in the tin for 5 minutes, then serve warm or transfer to a wire rack and leave to cool.

2
3

APRICOT & BANANA MUFFINS

Makes: 10 **Prep: 25–30 mins** **Cook: 25–30 mins**

Ingredients

- 225 g/8 oz self-raising wholemeal flour
- 2 tsp baking powder
- 25 g/1 oz light muscovado sugar
- 100 g/3½ oz ready-to-eat dried apricots, finely chopped
- 1 banana, mashed with 1 tbsp orange juice
- 1 tsp finely grated orange rind,
- 300 ml/10 fl oz skimmed milk
- 1 egg, beaten
- 3 tbsp corn oil
- 2 tbsp rolled oats

Method

1. Preheat the oven to 200°C/400°F/Gas Mark 6. Place 10 paper cases in a muffin tin. Sift the flour and baking powder into a mixing bowl, adding any husks that remain in the sieve. Stir in the sugar and chopped apricots.
2. Make a well in the centre of the dry ingredients and add the banana, orange rind, milk, beaten egg and oil. Mix together well to form a thick batter. Divide the mixture evenly between the paper cases.
3. Sprinkle each muffin with a few oats and bake in the preheated oven for 25–30 minutes, or until well risen and firm to the touch. Transfer the muffins to a wire rack to cool slightly. Serve the muffins warm.

TRAIL MIX

Serves: 12 **Prep: 10 mins** **Cook: N/A**

Ingredients

85 g/3 oz ready-to-eat dried apricots, chopped

85 g/3 oz dried cranberries

85 g/3 oz cashew nuts

85 g/3 oz hazelnuts

55 g/2 oz Brazil nuts, halved

55 g/2 oz flaked almonds

4 tbsp toasted pumpkin seeds

4 tbsp sunflower seeds

4 tbsp toasted pine nuts

Method

1 Put all the ingredients into a large bowl and mix well. Transfer to an airtight container until needed.

★ Variation

You can use any combination of dried fruits and nuts in this tasty recipe. Try adding raisins or dates instead of the dried cranberries or replace some of the nuts with pecans or walnuts. Try sprinkling it over breakfast cereals or keep a small pot in your bag for a tasty on-the-go snack.

BUDGET-BUSTING LUNCHES & SNACKS

ROASTED VEGETABLE & FETA CHEESE WRAPS

Serves: 4

Prep: 20–25 mins, plus cooling

Cook: 20–25 mins

Ingredients

1 red onion, cut into eighths

1 red pepper, cored and cut into eighths

1 small aubergine, cut into eighths

1 courgette, cut into eighths

4 tbsp extra virgin olive oil

1 garlic clove, crushed

100 g/3½ oz feta cheese, crumbled

small bunch of fresh mint, shredded

4 flour tortillas

salt and pepper

Method

1 Preheat the oven to 220°C/425°F/Gas Mark 7. Mix together the vegetables, oil, garlic and salt and pepper to taste in a non-stick baking sheet and place in the preheated oven. Roast for 15–20 minutes, or until golden and cooked through.

2 Remove from the oven and leave to cool. Once cool, mix in the feta and mint.

3 Preheat a non-stick frying pan until almost smoking. Add the tortillas and warm for a few seconds on each side. Remove from the pan.

4 Divide the vegetable and feta mixture between the tortillas. Fold the bottoms and tops of the tortillas over the filling, then roll up and cut in half. Serve immediately.

★ Variation

For an extra flavour dimension, spread the tortillas with a little hummus or tahini before topping with the roasted vegetables and cheese.

TURKEY SALAD PITTA

Serves: 1 **Prep: 15 mins** **Cook: 2 mins**

Ingredients

- small handful baby leaf spinach, shredded
- ½ red pepper, deseeded and thinly sliced
- ½ carrot, coarsely grated
- 4 tbsp hummus
- 85 g/3 oz boneless, skinless cooked turkey, thinly sliced
- ½ tbsp toasted sunflower seeds
- 1 wholemeal pitta bread
- salt and pepper

Method

1. Put the spinach, red pepper, carrot and hummus into a large bowl and stir together, so all the salad ingredients are coated with the hummus. Stir in the turkey and sunflower seeds and season to taste with salt and pepper.
2. Preheat the grill to medium. Put the pitta bread under the preheated grill for about 1 minute on each side to warm through, but do not brown. Cut it in half to make two 'pockets'.
3. Divide the salad, hummus and turkey mixture between the pitta pockets and serve.

CHICKEN SATAY SANDWICHES

Serves: 2 **Prep: 10–15 mins** **Cook: 2 mins**

Ingredients

2 heaped tbsp crunchy peanut butter

3 tbsp thick natural yogurt

150 g/5½ oz cooked Thai- or Chinese-style chicken strips

4 slices wholemeal bread

cucumber strips and salad leaves, to serve

Method

1. Place the peanut butter in a saucepan and cook over a medium heat, stirring all the time, until runny, or place in a microwavable jug or bowl and heat on medium in the microwave for around 20 seconds, or until runny.
2. Add the yogurt to the peanut butter and stir well to combine, then add the chicken strips and stir to coat with the dressing.
3. Spoon the chicken mixture onto two slices of the bread, then top with the remaining bread. Serve with cucumber strips and salad leaves.

WELSH RAREBIT

Serves: 2

Prep: 15 mins, plus cooling

Cook: 10–12 mins

Ingredients

- 4 slices thick brown bread
- 225 g/8 oz mature Cheddar cheese, grated
- 25 g/1 oz butter
- 3 tbsp beer
- ½ tsp mustard powder
- 1 egg, beaten
- salt and pepper

Method

1. Preheat the grill to medium. Toast the bread under the preheated grill on one side only.
2. Put the cheese into a saucepan and add the butter and beer. Heat slowly over a low heat, stirring continuously. Add some salt and pepper and the mustard powder and stir well until the mixture is thick and creamy. Remove from the heat and leave to cool slightly before mixing in the egg. Preheat the grill to high.
3. Spread the cheese mixture generously over the untoasted side of the bread and place under the hot grill until golden and bubbling. Serve immediately.

2
3

TUNA & SWEETCORN MELTS

Serves: 2 **Prep: 15 mins** **Cook: 5–6 mins**

Ingredients

2 wholemeal pitta breads

5 tbsp ready-made tomato pizza sauce

100 g/3½ oz canned tuna in water or oil, drained

50 g/1¾ oz canned, drained sweetcorn kernels

100 g/3½ oz mozzarella cheese, thinly sliced

Method

1 Preheat the grill to medium. Lightly sprinkle the pittas with water and toast one side until piping hot and springy to the touch.

2 Remove the grill pan from the grill, turn the pittas and spread them evenly with the tomato sauce, followed by the tuna and sweetcorn. Top with the cheese slices.

3 Return to the grill and cook until the cheese is bubbling and melted. Serve immediately.

MINI MUFFIN PIZZAS

Serves: 2 **Prep: 15–20 mins** **Cook: 8–10 mins**

Ingredients

2 tbsp tomato purée
2 tbsp pesto
3 wholemeal English muffins, split
1 tbsp olive oil
½ red onion, thinly sliced
3 mushrooms, sliced
½ courgette, thinly sliced
2–3 slices ham or 6 slices salami
100 g/3½ oz grated Cheddar cheese or 6 slices mozzarella cheese

Method

1. Mix together the tomato purée and pesto in a small bowl and spread equally over the muffin halves.
2. Heat the oil in a non-stick frying pan and then cook the onion, mushrooms and courgette until soft and beginning to brown.
3. Preheat the grill to high. Divide the vegetables between the muffins and top with the ham and then the cheese.
4. Cook under the preheated grill for 3–4 minutes, until the cheese is melted and browned. Serve hot or cold.

CHORIZO & CHEESE QUESADILLAS

Serves: 4 **Prep: 20 mins** **Cook: 25–30 mins**

Ingredients

- 115 g/4 oz mozzarella cheese, grated
- 115 g/4 oz Cheddar cheese, grated
- 225 g/8 oz cooked chorizo sausage (outer casing removed), diced
- 4 spring onions, finely chopped
- 2 fresh green chillies, deseeded and finely chopped
- 8 flour tortillas
- vegetable oil, for brushing
- salt and pepper
- guacamole and salsa, to serve

Method

1. Place the cheeses, chorizo, spring onions, chillies and salt and pepper to taste in a bowl and mix together. Divide the mixture between four of the tortillas, then top with the remaining tortillas.
2. Brush a large non-stick or heavy-based frying pan with oil and heat over a medium heat. Add one quesadilla and cook, pressing it down with a spatula, for 4–5 minutes, until the underside is crisp and lightly browned. Turn over and cook the other side until the cheese is melting. Remove from the frying pan and keep warm. Cook the remaining quesadillas.
3. Cut each quesadilla into quarters and serve with guacamole and salsa.

BAGELS WITH LEEKS & CHEESE

Serves: 2

Prep: 20 mins, plus cooling

Cook: 12 mins

Ingredients

2 leeks

25 g/1 oz butter

125 g/4½ oz Gruyère cheese, grated

2 spring onions, finely chopped

1 tbsp chopped fresh parsley

2 bagels

salt and pepper

Method

1 Trim the leeks, discarding the green ends, and split down the middle, leaving the root intact. Wash well to remove any grit and slice finely, discarding the root.

2 Melt the butter over a low heat in a large sauté pan and add the leeks. Cook, stirring constantly, for 5 minutes, or until the leeks are soft and slightly browned. Leave to cool.

3 Preheat the grill to medium. Mix together the cooled leeks, grated cheese, spring onions, parsley and salt and pepper to taste. Split the bagels and place under the preheated grill until lightly toasted on the bottoms. Spread the cheese mixture over the tops of the bagels and return to the grill until bubbling and golden brown. Serve immediately.

FRIED HAM & CHEESE SANDWICH

Serves: 1 **Prep: 10–15 mins** **Cook: 6–8 mins**

Ingredients

- 2 thin slices crusty bread
- 20 g/¾ oz butter, softened
- 55 g/2 oz Gruyère cheese, grated
- 1 slice cooked ham, trimmed to fit the bread, if necessary

Method

1. Thinly spread each slice of bread on one side with butter, then put one slice on the work surface, buttered side down.
2. Sprinkle half the cheese over the non-buttered side of bread, taking it to the edge. Add the ham and the remaining cheese, then top with the other slice of bread, buttered side up, and press down.
3. Heat a heavy-based frying pan over a medium–high heat. Reduce the heat to medium, add the sandwich and fry on one side for 2–3 minutes, until golden brown.
4. Flip the sandwich over and fry on the other side for 2–3 minutes, until all the cheese is melted and the bread is golden brown.
5. Cut the sandwich in half diagonally and serve immediately.

MIGHTY MEATBALL SUBS

Serves: 4

Prep: 25 mins, plus chilling

Cook: 25–30 mins

Ingredients

groundnut oil, for shallow-frying

1 tbsp olive oil

1 small onion, sliced

4 sub rolls or small baguettes

4 tbsp mayonnaise

55 g/2 oz sliced jalapeños (from a jar)

2 tbsp American mustard

Meatballs

450 g/1 lb fresh lean beef mince

1 small onion, grated

2 garlic cloves, crushed

25 g/1 oz fine white breadcrumbs

1 tsp hot chilli sauce

salt and pepper

wholemeal flour, for dusting

Method

1 For the meatballs, place the beef, onion, garlic, breadcrumbs and chilli sauce into a bowl. Season to taste with salt and pepper and mix thoroughly. Shape the mixture into 20 small equal-sized balls using floured hands. Cover and chill in the refrigerator for 10 minutes, or until required.

2 Heat a shallow depth of groundnut oil in a wok or heavy frying pan until very hot, then fry the meatballs in batches for 6–8 minutes, turning often, until golden brown and firm. Remove with a slotted spoon, drain on kitchen paper and keep hot.

3 Heat the olive oil in a clean pan and fry the onions over a medium heat, stirring occasionally, until soft and golden brown.

4 Split the rolls lengthways, without cutting all the way through, and spread with the mayonnaise. Arrange the onions, meatballs and jalapeños down the centre of the rolls and squeeze over the mustard. Serve immediately.

2
4

SUPER-SIZED FISH FINGER SANDWICHES

Serves: 2 **Prep: 15 mins** **Cook: 15 mins**

Ingredients

oil, for deep-frying
20 fish fingers
4 large slices white bread
100 g/3½ oz rocket

Russian dressing

2 tbsp mayonnaise
1 tbsp creamed horseradish
1 tbsp tomato ketchup
1 tbsp soured cream
1 tbsp sriracha hot chilli sauce
1 tsp Worcestershire sauce
½ tsp smoked paprika

Method

1 Mix together all of the Russian dressing ingredients in a small bowl and set aside.

2 Heat enough oil for deep-frying in a large pan or deep-fryer to 180–190°C/350–375°F, or until a cube of bread browns in 30 seconds.

3 Deep-fry the fish fingers in batches of ten for 5 minutes, or until golden. Remove with a slotted spoon, drain on kitchen paper and leave in a warm place while you cook the remaining fish fingers.

4 Spread the dressing over one side of each slice of bread. Divide the fish fingers between two of the slices, then top with the rocket and the remaining slices of bread. Serve immediately.

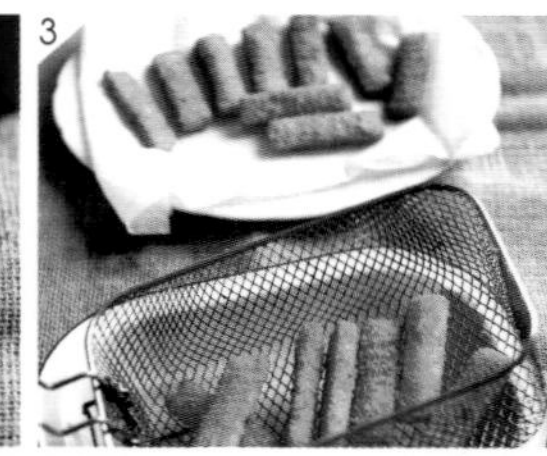
3

4

CREAMY SALMON BAKED POTATOES

Serves: 4 **Prep: 25 mins** **Cook: 1 hour 20 mins**

Ingredients

- 4 baking potatoes, about 275 g/9¾ oz each
- 250 g/9 oz skinless salmon fillet
- 200 g/7 oz soft cheese
- 2–3 tbsp milk
- 2 tbsp chopped fresh herbs, such as dill or chives
- 60 g/2¼ oz mature Cheddar cheese, grated
- salt and pepper

Method

1. Preheat the oven to 200°C/400°F/Gas Mark 6. Prick the skins of the potatoes and place on the top shelf of the preheated oven. Bake for 1¼ hours, until the skins are crisp and the centres are soft when pierced with a sharp knife or skewer.
2. Meanwhile, bring a saucepan of water to the boil, then reduce the heat until the water is simmering gently. Add the salmon fillet to the pan and cook for 4–5 minutes (if in one piece), or until just cooked but still moist. Using a fork, flake the flesh into a bowl.
3. In a separate bowl, blend the soft cheese with just enough of the milk to loosen, then stir in the herbs and a little salt and pepper.
4. When the potatoes are cooked, preheat the grill to high. Cut the potatoes in half lengthways. Carefully scoop the potato flesh out of the skins, reserving the skins. Add to the soft cheese mixture and mash together. Lightly stir in the salmon flakes.
5. Spoon the filling into the potato skins and top with the Cheddar cheese. Cook under the preheated grill for 1–2 minutes, until the cheese is bubbling and golden. Serve immediately.

POTATO SKINS WITH GUACAMOLE DIP

Serves: 4

Prep: 25 mins, plus cooling

Cook: 1 hour 25 mins

Ingredients

4 baking potatoes, about 225 g/8 oz each

2 tsp olive oil

salt and pepper

Guacamole dip

175 g/6 oz ripe avocado

1 tbsp lemon juice

2 tomatoes, finely chopped

1 tsp grated lemon rind

100 g/3½ oz low-fat soft cheese with garlic and herbs

4 spring onions, finely chopped

a few drops of hot pepper sauce

salt and pepper

Method

1. Preheat the oven to 200°C/400°F/Gas Mark 6. Prick the skins of the potatoes and place on the top shelf of the preheated oven. Bake for 1 hour, until the skins are crisp and the centres are soft when pierced with a sharp knife or skewer. Remove from the oven and allow to cool for 30 minutes. Reset the oven temperature to 220°C/425°F/Gas Mark 7.
2. Halve the potatoes lengthwise and scoop out 2 tablespoons of the flesh. Place the skins on a baking sheet and brush the flesh side lightly with the oil. Sprinkle with salt and pepper. Bake for a further 25 minutes, until golden and crisp. Drain on kitchen paper.
3. To make the guacamole dip, mash the avocado with the lemon juice. Add the remaining ingredients and mix well. Transfer to a serving bowl.
4. Serve the potato skins hot with the dip.

BABA GHANOUSH

Serves: 6

Prep: 20–25 mins, plus cooling

Cook: 1 hour

Ingredients

- 2 large aubergines
- 1 garlic clove, chopped
- 2 tsp ground cumin
- 4 tbsp tahini
- 2 tbsp lemon juice
- 4 tbsp natural yogurt
- 2 tbsp chopped fresh coriander, plus extra to garnish

Method

1. Preheat the oven to 220°C/425°F/Gas Mark 7. Prick the aubergine skins and place them on a baking sheet. Bake for 1 hour, or until very soft. Remove from the oven and set aside to cool.
2. Peel off and discard the aubergine skins. Coarsely chop the flesh and place it in a food processor. Add the garlic, cumin, tahini, lemon juice, yogurt and chopped coriander and process until smooth and combined, scraping down the sides as necessary.
3. Transfer to a serving dish, sprinkle with a little chopped coriander and serve.

HUMMUS

Serves: 6 **Prep: 20 mins** **Cook: N/A**

Ingredients

400 g/14 oz canned chickpeas, drained and rinsed

1 garlic clove, crushed to a paste with ¼ tsp salt

3–4 tbsp tahini

2–4 tbsp lemon juice

¼ tsp ground cumin

extra virgin olive oil (optional), plus extra to serve

salt

paprika and chopped fresh parsley, to garnish

Method

1 Put all but 1 tablespoon of the chickpeas into a food processor. Add the garlic and process to a thick, coarse paste. Add 3 tablespoons of the tahini and process again until blended. Add 2 tablespoons of the lemon juice, the cumin and salt to taste and process until creamy. Taste and add extra tahini and/or lemon juice, if desired. For a thinner dip, with the motor running, drizzle in oil or water until you reach the desired consistency.

2 To serve, transfer to a serving bowl, then use the back of a spoon to make an indentation in the centre of the dip. Put the reserved chickpeas in the indentation and drizzle with oil. Sprinkle with paprika and chopped parsley to garnish.

SPICED BEETROOT & CUCUMBER TZATZIKI

Serves: 4 **Prep: 15–20 mins** **Cook: N/A**

Ingredients

115 g/4 oz cooked beetroot in natural juices (drained weight), drained and diced

150 g/5½ oz cucumber, diced

40 g/1½ oz radishes, diced

1 spring onion, finely chopped

12 Little Gem lettuce leaves

Dressing

150 g/5½ oz 2 percent fat Greek-style natural yogurt

¼ tsp ground cumin

½ tsp honey

2 tbsp finely chopped fresh mint

salt and pepper

Method

1. To make the dressing, put the yogurt, cumin and honey in a bowl, then stir in the mint and season to taste with salt and pepper.
2. Add the beetroot, cucumber, radishes and spring onion, then toss gently together.
3. Arrange the lettuce leaves on a plate. Spoon a little of the salad into each leaf. Serve immediately.

SMOKED MACKEREL PÂTÉ

Serves: 4

Prep: 20 mins, plus chilling

Cook: 6–8 mins

Ingredients

250 g/9 oz smoked mackerel fillets, skinned and any small bones removed, flaked

125 g/4½ oz silken tofu

2 tbsp lemon juice

1 tsp grated horseradish (optional)

1 tbsp chopped fresh dill or snipped fresh chives, plus extra to garnish

4 slices wholemeal bread

pepper

Method

1 Put the mackerel, tofu, lemon juice and horseradish, if using, in a food processor or blender and process until smooth. Add pepper to taste. You will not need salt because the mackerel is salty enough.

2 Stir in the fresh herbs, then transfer to a bowl, cover and chill until about 10 minutes before serving. Sprinkle over some fresh herbs.

3 Meanwhile, preheat the grill to high. Toast the bread on both sides until just golden brown. Using a long, serrated knife, cut off the crusts, then thinly slice each piece of toast horizontally through the centre. Cut each piece into two triangles, then toast the untoasted sides until they are golden and the edges have curled up. Serve with the pâté.

COUSCOUS SALAD WITH ROASTED BUTTERNUT SQUASH

Serves: 4 **Prep: 25–30 mins** **Cook: 30–40 mins**

Ingredients

2 tbsp honey

4 tbsp olive oil

1 butternut squash, peeled, deseeded and cut into 2-cm/¾-inch chunks

250 g/9 oz couscous

400 ml/14 fl oz hot vegetable stock

½ cucumber, diced

1 courgette, diced

1 red pepper, deseeded and diced

juice of ½ lemon

2 tbsp chopped fresh parsley

salt and pepper

Method

1 Preheat the oven to 190°C/375°F/Gas Mark 5. Mix half the honey with 1 tablespoon of the oil in a large bowl, add the squash and toss well to coat. Tip into a roasting tin and roast in the preheated oven for 30–40 minutes, until soft and golden.

2 Meanwhile, put the couscous in a heatproof bowl. Pour the stock over the couscous, cover and leave to stand for 3 minutes. Add 1 tablespoon of the remaining oil and fork through, then stir in the cucumber, courgette and red pepper. Re-cover and keep warm.

3 Whisk the remaining honey and oil with the lemon juice in a jug and season to taste with salt and pepper. Stir the mixture into the couscous.

4 To serve, top the couscous with the roasted squash and sprinkle with the parsley.

PASTA SALAD WITH CHARGRILLED PEPPERS

Serves: 4 **Prep: 20 mins** **Cook: 15 mins**

Ingredients

1 red pepper
1 orange pepper
280 g/10 oz dried conchiglie
5 tbsp extra virgin olive oil
2 tbsp lemon juice
2 tbsp pesto
1 garlic clove, crushed
3 tbsp shredded fresh basil leaves
salt and pepper

Method

1 Put the whole peppers on a baking sheet and place under a preheated grill, turning frequently, for 15 minutes, until charred all over. Remove with tongs and place in a bowl. Cover with crumpled kitchen paper and set aside.

2 Meanwhile, bring a large, heavy-based saucepan of lightly salted water to the boil. Add the pasta, bring back to the boil and cook for 8–10 minutes, until tender but still firm to the bite.

3 Combine the oil, lemon juice, pesto and garlic in a large bowl, whisking well to mix. Drain the pasta, add it to the pesto mixture while still hot and toss well. Set aside.

4 When the peppers are cool enough to handle, peel off the skins, then cut open and remove the seeds. Chop the flesh roughly and add to the pasta with the basil. Season to taste with salt and pepper and toss well. Serve at room temperature.

HERBY POTATO SALAD

Serves: 4

Prep: 20 mins, plus cooling

Cook: 15 mins

Ingredients

- 500 g/1 lb 2 oz new potatoes
- 16 cherry tomatoes, halved
- 55 g/2 oz black olives, pitted and roughly chopped
- 4 spring onions, finely sliced
- 2 tbsp chopped fresh mint
- 2 tbsp chopped fresh parsley
- 2 tbsp chopped fresh coriander
- juice of 1 lemon
- 3 tbsp extra virgin olive oil
- salt and pepper

Method

1. Cook the potatoes in a saucepan of lightly salted boiling water for 15 minutes, or until tender. Drain, then cool slightly before peeling off the skins. Cut into halves or quarters, depending on the size of the potato.
2. Combine the potatoes with the tomatoes, olives, spring onions and herbs in a salad bowl.
3. Mix the lemon juice and oil together in a small bowl or jug and pour over the potato salad. Season to taste with salt and pepper before serving.

BANG BANG CHICKEN SALAD

Serves: 4 **Prep: 20 mins** **Cook: 3–5 mins**

Ingredients

225 g/8 oz Chinese leaves, roughly torn

2 carrots, cut into thin sticks

½ cucumber, deseeded and cut into thin sticks

55 g/2 oz beansprouts

400 g/14 oz cooked boneless chicken breast, shredded

1 tbsp toasted sesame seeds

1 tbsp chopped salted peanuts

Dressing

4 tbsp smooth peanut butter

2 tbsp sweet chilli sauce

1 tbsp soy sauce

1 tbsp rice vinegar

1 tbsp sunflower oil

1 tbsp roasted peanut oil

Method

1 To make the dressing, place the peanut butter in a heatproof bowl. Set the bowl over a saucepan of simmering water and stir until the peanut butter has melted. Stir in the chilli sauce, soy sauce and rice vinegar. Remove from the heat and gradually stir in the sunflower and peanut oils to make a dressing with a smooth pouring consistency.

2 Place the Chinese leaves in a large bowl with the carrots, cucumber and beansprouts. Top with the shredded chicken and spoon over the warm dressing. Toss well.

3 Sprinkle with the sesame seeds and peanuts just before serving.

LENTIL & TUNA SALAD

Serves: 4 **Prep: 20 mins** **Cook: N/A**

Ingredients

- 2 ripe tomatoes
- 1 small red onion
- small bunch of fresh coriander
- 400 g/14 oz canned green lentils, drained
- 185 g/6½ oz canned tuna in spring water, drained
- pepper

Dressing

- 3 tbsp virgin olive oil
- 1 tbsp lemon juice
- 1 tsp wholegrain mustard
- 1 garlic clove, crushed
- ½ tsp ground cumin
- ½ tsp ground coriander

Method

1. Using a sharp knife, deseed the tomatoes and chop them into small dice. Finely chop the red onion and the fresh coriander.
2. To make the dressing, whisk together the oil, lemon juice, mustard, garlic, cumin and ground coriander in a small bowl until thoroughly combined. Set aside until required.
3. Mix together the chopped onion, diced tomatoes and drained lentils in a large bowl.
4. Flake the tuna with a fork and stir it into the onion, tomato and lentil mixture. Stir in the coriander and mix well.
5. Pour the dressing over the lentil and tuna salad and season to taste with pepper. Serve immediately.

1
1
1

CHICKEN NOODLE SOUP

Serves: 6 **Prep: 15 mins** **Cook: 35–40 mins**

Ingredients

- 2 skinless, boneless chicken breasts
- 1.2 litres/2 pints water or chicken stock
- 3 carrots, sliced into 5-mm/¼-inch slices
- 85 g/3 oz egg noodles
- salt and pepper
- fresh tarragon leaves, to garnish (optional)

Method

1. Place the chicken breasts in a large saucepan over a medium heat, add the water and bring to a simmer. Cook for 25–30 minutes. Skim any foam from the surface, if necessary. Remove the chicken from the cooking liquid and keep warm.
2. Continue to simmer the cooking liquid, add the carrots and noodles and cook for 4–5 minutes.
3. Thinly slice or shred the chicken breasts and place in warmed serving bowls.
4. Season the soup with salt and pepper to taste and pour over the chicken. Serve immediately, garnished with the tarragon, if using.

HAM & LENTIL SOUP

Serves: 2 **Prep: 15 mins** **Cook: 25 mins**

Ingredients

- 200 g/7 oz cooked ham
- 1 tbsp vegetable oil
- 1 onion, finely chopped
- 1 garlic clove, finely chopped
- 1 carrot, finely diced
- 1 celery stick, thinly sliced
- 400 g/14 oz canned green lentils, drained and rinsed
- 1 tsp finely chopped fresh rosemary leaves
- 600 ml/1 pint vegetable stock or ham stock
- pepper

Method

1. Using two forks, finely shred the cooked ham and set aside.
2. Heat the oil in a saucepan over a medium–high heat. Add the onion, garlic, carrot and celery and sauté for 4–5 minutes, or until starting to soften.
3. Add the lentils, rosemary, shredded ham and stock, and season to taste with pepper. Cover and simmer for 20 minutes, or until the vegetables are just tender. Serve immediately.

SCOTCH BROTH

Serves: 8

Prep: 25–30 mins, plus cooling & chilling

Cook: 2 hours 20 mins

Ingredients

- 700 g/1 lb 9 oz neck of lamb
- 1.7 litres/3 pints water
- 55 g/2 oz pearl barley
- 2 onions, chopped
- 1 garlic clove, finely chopped
- 3 small turnips, diced
- 3 carrots, finely sliced
- 2 celery sticks, sliced
- 2 leeks, sliced
- salt and pepper
- 2 tbsp chopped fresh parsley, to garnish

Method

1. Cut the meat into chunks, removing as much fat as possible.
2. Put the meat into a large saucepan and cover with the water. Bring to the boil over a medium heat and skim off any foam that appears. Add the pearl barley, reduce the heat and cook gently, covered, for 1 hour.
3. Add the onion, garlic and vegetables and season with salt and pepper to taste. Continue to cook for a further hour.
4. Remove the meat from the saucepan using a slotted spoon and strip the meat from the bones. Discard the bones and any fat or gristle. Place the meat back in the saucepan and leave to cool thoroughly, then refrigerate overnight.
5. Scrape the solidified fat off the surface of the soup. Reheat, season with salt and pepper to taste and ladle into bowls. Serve immediately, garnished with the parsley.

CHUNKY VEGETABLE SOUP

Serves: 4 **Prep: 15 mins** **Cook: 20–25 mins**

Ingredients

1 red onion
1 celery stick
1 courgette
2 carrots
2 tbsp sunflower oil
400 g/14 oz canned chopped plum tomatoes
300 ml/10 fl oz chicken stock or vegetable stock
large fresh thyme sprig, plus extra chopped thyme to garnish
salt and pepper

Method

1. Cut the onion, celery, courgette and carrots into 1-cm/½-inch cubes.
2. Heat the oil in a large saucepan over a medium heat. Add the vegetables and sauté, stirring, for 5 minutes without browning.
3. Add the tomatoes, stock and the thyme sprig. Bring to the boil, then reduce the heat. Cover and simmer for 10–15 minutes, until the vegetables are just tender. Remove the thyme sprig and season to taste with salt and pepper.
4. Transfer the soup to warmed serving bowls. Garnish with chopped thyme and serve immediately.

1
2
3

CARROT & CORIANDER SOUP

Serves: 6 **Prep: 15 mins** **Cook: 45 mins**

Ingredients

3 tbsp olive oil

1 red onion, chopped

1 large potato, chopped

1 celery stick, chopped

500 g/1 lb 2 oz carrots, chopped

1 litre/1¾ pints vegetable stock

25 g/1 oz butter

2 tsp coriander seeds, crushed

1½ tbsp chopped fresh coriander, plus extra to garnish

225 ml/8 fl oz milk

salt and pepper

Method

1. Heat the oil in a large saucepan. Add the onion and cook over a low heat, stirring occasionally, for 5 minutes, until softened.
2. Add the potato and celery and cook, stirring occasionally, for 5 minutes, then add the carrots and cook for a further 5 minutes. Cover the pan, reduce the heat to very low and cook, shaking the pan occasionally, for 10 minutes.
3. Pour in the stock and bring to the boil, then cover and simmer for 10 minutes, until the vegetables are tender.
4. Meanwhile, melt the butter in a frying pan. Add the coriander seeds and cook, stirring constantly, for 1 minute. Add the chopped coriander and cook, stirring constantly, for 1 minute, then remove from the heat.
5. Purée the soup in the pan with a hand-held blender until smooth. Stir in the coriander mixture and milk and season to taste with salt and pepper. Reheat gently. Sprinkle with chopped coriander and serve.

2
4
5

ROASTED SQUASH SOUP WITH CHEESE TOASTIES

Serves: 4 **Prep: 25–30 mins** **Cook: 1 hour 5 mins–1¼ hours**

Ingredients

1 kg/2 lb 4 oz butternut squash, cut into small chunks

2 onions, cut into wedges

2 tbsp olive oil

2 garlic cloves, crushed

3–4 fresh thyme sprigs, leaves removed

1 litre/1¾ pints vegetable stock

150 ml/5 fl oz crème fraîche

salt and pepper

snipped fresh chives, to garnish

Toasties

1 baguette, thinly sliced diagonally

40 g/1½ oz Cheddar cheese, grated

Method

1 Preheat the oven to 190°C/375°F/Gas Mark 5. Place the squash, onions, oil, garlic and thyme leaves in a roasting tin. Toss together and spread out in a single layer. Roast for 50–60 minutes, stirring occasionally, until tender.

2 Transfer the vegetables to a saucepan. Add half the stock and purée with a hand-held blender until smooth. Stir in the remaining stock and the crème fraîche. Season to taste with salt and pepper, and heat through gently.

3 To make the toasties, preheat the grill to high. Toast the sliced baguette under the preheated grill for 1–2 minutes on each side, until pale golden in colour. Sprinkle with the cheese and return to the grill until melted and bubbling.

4 Ladle the soup into bowls, sprinkle with chives and serve with the cheese toasties.

★ Variation

Try using pumpkin in place of the squash and garnish with pumpkin seeds instead of the chives.

HOME COMFORTS JUST LIKE MUM MAKES

CHILLI CON CARNE

Serves: 4 **Prep: 15 mins** **Cook: 25 mins**

Ingredients

200 g/7 oz basmati rice
2 tbsp olive oil
1 large onion, sliced
500 g/1 lb 2 oz fresh lean beef mince
1 garlic clove, crushed
400 g/14 oz canned chopped tomatoes
400 g/14 oz canned red kidney beans, drained and rinsed
200 ml/7 fl oz beef stock
2 tbsp tomato purée
2 tsp crushed dried chillies
salt and pepper

Method

1 Cook the rice in a saucepan of lightly salted water for 10–12 minutes, until tender. Drain.

2 Meanwhile, heat the oil in a large saucepan over a high heat, add the onion and beef and fry, stirring frequently and breaking up the beef with a wooden spoon, until the beef is evenly browned.

3 Stir in the garlic, then add the tomatoes, beans, stock, tomato purée and chillies. Stir until boiling, then reduce the heat, cover and simmer for 15 minutes, stirring occasionally. Season to taste with salt and pepper.

4 Serve immediately with the rice.

★ Variation

To make this meal go even further, add 400 g/14 oz canned, drained chickpeas along with the red kidney beans in step 3.

MEATLOAF

Serves: 6–8

Prep: 25–30 mins, **plus cooling**

Cook: 1¼ hours– 1 hour 25 mins, **plus resting**

Ingredients

- 25 g/1 oz butter
- 1 tbsp olive oil, plus extra for brushing
- 3 garlic cloves, finely chopped
- 100 g/3½ oz carrots, very finely diced
- 55 g/2 oz celery, very finely diced
- 1 onion, very finely diced
- 1 red pepper, deseeded and very finely diced
- 4 large white mushrooms, very finely diced
- 1 tsp dried thyme
- 2 tsp finely chopped fresh rosemary
- 1 tsp Worcestershire sauce
- 6 tbsp tomato ketchup
- ½ tsp cayenne pepper
- 1.1 kg/2 lb 8 oz fresh beef mince, chilled
- 2 eggs, beaten
- 55 g/2 oz fresh breadcrumbs
- 2 tbsp brown sugar
- 1 tbsp Dijon mustard
- salt and pepper

Method

1. Melt the butter with the oil and garlic in a large frying pan. Add the vegetables and cook over a medium heat, stirring frequently, for 10 minutes, until most of the moisture has evaporated. Remove from the heat and stir in the herbs, Worcestershire sauce, 4 tablespoons of the ketchup and the cayenne pepper. Leave to cool.
2. Preheat the oven to 160°C/325°F/Gas Mark 3. Brush a loaf tin with oil.
3. Put the beef into a large bowl and gently break it up with your fingertips. Add the vegetable mixture, eggs and salt and pepper to taste and mix gently with your fingers. Add the breadcrumbs and mix. Transfer the meatloaf mixture to the loaf tin. Smooth the surface and bake in the preheated oven for 30 minutes.
4. Meanwhile, make a glaze by whisking together the sugar, the remaining 2 tablespoons of ketchup, the mustard and a pinch of salt.
5. Remove the meatloaf from the oven and spread the glaze evenly over the top. Bake for a further 35–45 minutes, until cooked through. Remove from the oven and leave to rest for at least 15 minutes before serving. Slice thickly to serve.

HOME COMFORTS JUST LIKE MUM MAKES

1
3
5

QUICK BEEF STEW

Serves: 4 **Prep: 20 mins** **Cook: 35 mins**

Ingredients

900 g/2 lb sliced stir-fry beef
3 tbsp plain flour
2 tbsp olive oil
1 large onion, diced
2 garlic cloves, finely chopped
225 ml/8 fl oz red wine
450 g/1 lb button mushrooms, quartered
450 g/1 lb new potatoes, diced
4 carrots, diced
2 celery sticks, diced
700 ml/1¼ pints beef stock
3 tbsp tomato purée
1 tbsp finely chopped fresh thyme leaves
2 tbsp finely chopped fresh parsley
salt and pepper

Method

1 Season the beef with ½ teaspoon salt and ½ teaspoon pepper. Toss in the flour.

2 Heat the oil in a large, heavy-based saucepan over a medium–high heat. Add the meat and cook, stirring frequently, for about 4 minutes, until brown all over. Add the onion and garlic to the pan and cook for 2–3 minutes, until the onion begins to soften. Add the wine and bring to the boil, scraping up any sediment from the base of the pan.

3 Add the vegetables to the pan with 1 teaspoon salt, ½ teaspoon pepper, the stock, tomato purée and thyme. Bring to the boil, then reduce the heat to low, cover, and simmer for about 15 minutes, until the vegetables are tender.

4 Remove the lid of the pan and continue to simmer for a further 5 minutes, until the sauce is slightly thickened. Stir the parsley into the pan. Taste and adjust the seasoning, adding salt and pepper if needed. Serve the stew hot.

2
3

POT ROAST

Serves: 6 **Prep: 30 mins** **Cook: 3 hours 40 mins**

Ingredients

2½ tbsp plain flour
1 rolled brisket joint, weighing 1.6 kg/3 lb 8 oz
2 tbsp vegetable oil
25 g/1 oz butter
1 onion, finely chopped
2 celery sticks, diced
2 carrots, diced
1 tsp dill seed
1 tsp dried thyme
350 ml/12 fl oz red wine
140–225 ml/5–8 fl oz beef stock
4–5 potatoes, cut into large chunks and parboiled
salt and pepper
2 tbsp chopped fresh dill, to serve

Method

1 Preheat the oven to 140°C/275°F/Gas Mark 1. Mix 2 tablespoons of the flour with 1 teaspoon salt and ¼ teaspoon pepper in a large shallow dish. Dip the meat in the flour to coat.

2 Heat the oil in a flameproof casserole over a medium heat, add the meat and brown. Transfer to a plate. Add half the butter to the casserole, then add the onion, celery, carrots, dill seed and thyme and cook for 5 minutes.

3 Return the meat and juices to the casserole. Pour in the wine and enough stock to reach one third of the way up the meat and bring to the boil.

4 Cover and cook in the preheated oven for 3 hours, turning the meat every 30 minutes. Add the potatoes and more stock after 2 hours, if necessary.

5 Transfer the meat and vegetables to a warmed serving dish. Strain the cooking liquid to remove any solids, then return the liquid to the casserole. Bring the cooking liquid to the boil over a medium–high heat. Mix the remaining butter and flour to a paste, then add small pieces of the paste to the cooking liquid, whisking constantly until smooth. Pour the sauce over the meat and vegetables. Sprinkle with dill and serve.

SLOPPY JOES

Serves: 4 **Prep: 15–20 mins** **Cook: 40 mins**

Ingredients

- 450 g/1 lb fresh beef mince
- 1 onion, chopped
- 1 garlic clove, chopped
- 1 green pepper, deseeded and chopped
- 1 tbsp American mustard
- 175 ml/6 fl oz tomato ketchup
- 1 tsp white vinegar
- 1 tbsp brown sugar
- pinch of chilli powder, ground cloves or paprika (optional)
- 4 burger buns, split
- salt and pepper

Method

1. Put the beef, onion, garlic and green pepper into a non-stick frying pan and cook over a medium heat, stirring frequently and breaking up the beef with a wooden spoon, for 8–10 minutes, until the beef is evenly browned. Carefully drain off the fat.
2. Stir in the mustard, ketchup, vinegar, sugar and chilli powder, if using. Season to taste with salt and pepper. Reduce the heat and simmer, stirring occasionally, for 30 minutes.
3. Divide the mixture among the burger buns and serve immediately.

STEAK & ENGLISH MUSTARD SANDWICHES

Serves: 2

Prep: 15–20 mins

Cook: 25–30 mins, plus resting

Ingredients

15 g/½ oz butter

2 tbsp olive oil

1 onion, halved and thinly sliced

½ tsp brown sugar

2 rump steaks, about 175 g/6 oz each and 2 cm/¾ inch thick

1 tsp coarsely ground black pepper

4 tbsp mayonnaise

2 tsp ready-made English mustard

4 slices thick crusty bread

25 g/1 oz rocket leaves

salt and pepper

Method

1. Heat the butter and half the oil in a frying pan and fry the onion gently for 10 minutes, until softened. Season to taste with salt and pepper and sprinkle over the sugar. Increase the heat a little and continue cooking for a further 5 minutes, until golden and caramelized.
2. Heat a cast-iron griddle pan until very hot. Drizzle the remaining oil over the steaks, coat with the black pepper and season lightly with salt. Add the steaks to the pan and cook over a high heat for 3–5 minutes on each side, until cooked to your liking. Remove the steaks from the pan, cover and leave to rest in a warm place for 10 minutes.
3. Mix together the mayonnaise and mustard and spread thickly over two slices of the bread. Top with the rocket leaves. Using a sharp knife, thinly slice the steaks at an angle. Pile the steak on top of the rocket leaves and top with the caramelized onions. Sandwich with the remaining slices of bread, and serve immediately.

PORK CHOPS WITH APPLE SAUCE

Serves: 4 **Prep: 20 mins** **Cook: 20–25 mins, plus standing**

Ingredients

4 pork rib chops on the bone, each about 3 cm/1¼ inches thick, at room temperature

1½ tbsp sunflower oil

salt and pepper

Chunky apple sauce

450 g/1 lb cooking apples, such as Bramley, peeled, cored and diced

4 tbsp caster sugar, plus extra if needed

finely grated rind of ½ lemon

½ tbsp lemon juice, plus extra if needed

4 tbsp water

¼ tsp ground cinnamon

knob of butter

Method

1 Preheat the oven to 200°C/400°F/Gas Mark 6.

2 For the apple sauce, put the apples, sugar, lemon rind, lemon juice and water into a heavy-based saucepan over a high heat and bring to the boil, stirring to dissolve the sugar. Reduce the heat to low, cover and simmer for 15–20 minutes, until the apples are tender. Stir in the cinnamon and butter and beat the apples until they are as smooth or chunky as you like. Stir in extra sugar or lemon juice, to taste. Remove the pan from the heat and cover to keep warm.

3 Meanwhile, pat the chops dry and season to taste with salt and pepper. Heat the oil in a large ovenproof frying pan over a medium–high heat. Add the chops and fry for 3 minutes on each side to brown.

4 Transfer the pan to the oven and roast the chops for 7–9 minutes, until cooked through. Remove the pan from the oven, cover with foil and leave to stand for 3 minutes. Gently reheat the apple sauce, if necessary.

5 Transfer the chops to plates, spoon over the pan juices and serve with the apple sauce.

ROAST CHICKEN

Serves: 6

Prep: 20 mins

Cook: 2 hours 5 mins, plus resting

Ingredients

1 chicken, weighing 2.25 kg/5 lb

55 g/2 oz butter, softened

2 tbsp chopped fresh lemon thyme, plus extra sprigs to garnish

1 lemon, cut into quarters

125 ml/4 fl oz white wine

salt and pepper

Method

1 Preheat the oven to 220°C/425°F/Gas Mark 7. Place the chicken in a roasting tin.

2 Put the butter in a bowl, then mix in the chopped thyme, and salt and pepper to taste. Use to butter the chicken.

3 Place the lemon inside the cavity. Pour over the wine and roast in the preheated oven for 15 minutes.

4 Reduce the oven temperature to 190°C/375°F/Gas Mark 5 and roast, basting frequently, for a further 1¾ hours.

5 To check a whole bird is cooked through, pierce the thickest part of the leg between the drumstick and the thigh with a thin skewer. Any juices should be piping hot and clear with no traces of red or pink. To further check, gently pull the leg away from the body, the leg should 'give' and no traces of pinkness or blood should remain. Transfer the chicken to a warmed platter, cover with foil and allow to rest for 10 minutes.

6 Place the roasting tin on the hob and simmer the pan juices gently over a low heat until they have reduced and are thick and glossy. Season to taste with salt and pepper and reserve.

7 To carve the chicken, place on a clean chopping board. Using a carving knife and fork, cut between the wings and the side of the breast. Remove the wings and cut slices off the breast. Cut the legs from the body and cut through the joint to make drumsticks and thigh portions.

8 Serve the chicken with the pan juices, garnished with thyme sprigs.

CHICKEN PIE

Serves: 4 **Prep: 20 mins** **Cook: 25–30 mins**

Ingredients

- 2 tbsp olive oil
- 450 g/1 lb chicken breast strips
- 175 g/6 oz baby button mushrooms
- 1 bunch spring onions, chopped
- 115 g/4 oz crème fraîche
- 4 tbsp chicken stock
- 375 g/13 oz ready-rolled shortcrust pastry
- beaten egg or milk, to glaze
- salt and pepper

Method

1. Preheat the oven to 220°C/425°F/Gas Mark 7. Place a baking sheet in the oven to preheat.
2. Heat the oil in a large frying pan over a high heat. Add the chicken and cook for 2–3 minutes, stirring frequently. Add the mushrooms and spring onions and cook for a further 2 minutes.
3. Add the crème fraîche, stock, and salt and pepper to taste, then tip into a 1.4-litre/2½-pint shallow, ovenproof dish.
4. Lift the pastry on top, scrunching the edges in with your fingers to fit inside the rim of the dish. Make a small slit in the centre and brush with beaten egg to glaze.
5. Place the dish on the preheated baking sheet and bake for 20–25 minutes, until the pastry is golden and firm. Transfer to warmed serving plates and serve immediately.

2
2
3

CHICKEN TAGINE

Serves: 4 **Prep: 20 mins** **Cook: 35–40 mins**

Ingredients

- 1 tbsp olive oil
- 1 onion, cut into small wedges
- 2–4 garlic cloves, sliced
- 450 g/1 lb skinless, boneless chicken breast, diced
- 1 tsp ground cumin
- 2 cinnamon sticks, lightly bruised
- 1 tbsp plain wholemeal flour
- 225 g/8 oz aubergine, diced
- 1 red pepper, deseeded and chopped
- 85 g/3 oz button mushrooms, sliced
- 1 tbsp tomato purée
- 600 ml/1 pint chicken stock
- 280 g/10 oz canned chickpeas, drained and rinsed
- 55 g/2 oz ready-to-eat dried apricots, chopped
- salt and pepper
- 1 tbsp chopped fresh coriander, to garnish

Method

1. Heat the oil in a large, deep frying pan over a medium heat, add the onion and garlic and cook for 3 minutes, stirring frequently. Add the chicken and cook, stirring constantly, for a further 5 minutes, or until sealed on all sides. Add the cumin and cinnamon sticks to the pan halfway through sealing the chicken.
2. Sprinkle in the flour and cook, stirring constantly, for 2 minutes.
3. Add the aubergine, red pepper and mushrooms and cook for 2 minutes, stirring constantly. Blend the tomato purée with the stock, stir into the pan and bring to the boil. Reduce the heat and add the chickpeas and apricots. Cover and simmer for 15–20 minutes, or until the chicken is tender.
4. Season to taste with salt and pepper and serve immediately, sprinkled with coriander.

CHICKEN KIEVS

Makes: 8

Prep: 30 mins, plus chilling

Cook: 25–30 mins

Ingredients

- 115 g/4 oz butter, softened
- 3–4 garlic cloves, very finely chopped
- 1 tbsp chopped fresh parsley
- 1 tbsp snipped fresh chives
- juice and finely grated rind of ½ lemon
- 8 skinless, boneless chicken breasts, about 115 g/4 oz each
- 55 g/2 oz plain flour
- 2 eggs, lightly beaten
- 175 g/6 oz dry breadcrumbs
- groundnut oil or sunflower oil, for deep-frying
- salt and pepper

Method

1. Beat the butter in a bowl with the garlic, herbs, and lemon juice and rind. Season to taste with salt and pepper. Divide into eight pieces, then shape into cylinders. Wrap in foil and chill in the refrigerator until firm.
2. Place each chicken breast between two sheets of clingfilm. Pound gently with a meat mallet or rolling pin to flatten the chicken to an even thickness. Place a butter cylinder on each chicken piece and roll up. Secure with cocktail sticks.
3. Place the flour, eggs and breadcrumbs in separate shallow dishes. Dip the rolls into the flour, then the egg and, finally, the breadcrumbs. Chill in the refrigerator for 1 hour.
4. Heat enough oil for deep-frying in a saucepan or deep-fat fryer to 180–190°C/350–375°F, or until a cube of bread browns in 30 seconds. Deep-fry the chicken, in batches, for 8–10 minutes, or until cooked through and golden brown. Drain on kitchen paper and remove the cocktail sticks. Serve immediately.

1
2
3

CAJUN CHICKEN

Serves: 2 **Prep: 20 mins** **Cook: 30–35 mins**

Ingredients

4 chicken drumsticks
4 chicken thighs
2 fresh sweetcorn cobs, husks and silks removed
85 g/3 oz butter, melted
oil, for cooking

Spice mix

2 tsp onion powder
2 tsp paprika
1½ tsp salt
1 tsp garlic powder
1 tsp dried thyme
1 tsp cayenne pepper
1 tsp ground black pepper
½ tsp ground white pepper
¼ tsp ground cumin

Method

1 Using a sharp knife, make two to three diagonal slashes in the chicken drumsticks and thighs, then place them in a large dish. Add the corn cobs. Mix together all the ingredients for the spice mix in a small bowl.

2 Brush the chicken and corn with the melted butter and sprinkle with the spice mix. Toss to coat well.

3 Heat the oil in a large griddle pan over a medium–high heat and cook the chicken, turning occasionally, for 15 minutes, then add the sweetcorn cobs and cook, turning occasionally, for a further 10–15 minutes, or until beginning to blacken slightly at the edges. Check the chicken is tender and the juices run clear when a skewer is inserted into the thickest part of the meat. Transfer to a serving plate and serve.

TURKEY SCHNITZEL WITH POTATO WEDGES

Serves: 4 **Prep: 20–25 mins** **Cook: 35 mins**

Ingredients

4 potatoes
2 tbsp olive oil, plus extra for shallow-frying
3 tsp dried sage
55 g/2 oz fresh breadcrumbs
40 g/1½ oz finely grated Parmesan cheese
4 thinly sliced turkey escalopes
1 egg, beaten
salt and pepper

Method

1 Preheat the oven to 220°C/425°F/Gas Mark 7. Cut each potato into eight wedges. Place the potatoes, oil and 1 teaspoon of the sage into a large mixing bowl. Season to taste with salt and pepper and turn to coat evenly. Arrange the potatoes in a single layer on a baking sheet. Bake in the preheated oven for 25 minutes, until golden brown and tender.

2 Meanwhile, place the breadcrumbs, cheese and the remaining sage into a wide, shallow dish. Season to taste with salt and pepper and mix together. Dip the turkey in the beaten egg and then in the breadcrumb mixture, pressing to coat on both sides.

3 Heat a shallow depth of oil in a frying pan over a fairly high heat, add the turkey and fry for 4–5 minutes, turning once, until the turkey is tender and cooked through.

4 Serve the turkey schnitzel immediately with the potato wedges.

STEAMED SALMON

Serves: 4 **Prep: 15–20 mins** **Cook: 22 mins**

Ingredients

- 40 g/1½ oz butter, melted
- 4 salmon fillets, about 140 g/5 oz each
- juice and finely grated rind of 1 lemon
- 1 tbsp snipped fresh chives
- 1 tbsp chopped fresh parsley
- salt and pepper
- salad and crusty bread, to serve

Method

1. Preheat the oven to 200°/400°F/Gas Mark 6. Cut four 30-cm/12-inch squares of double thickness foil and brush with the melted butter.
2. Place a piece of salmon on each square and spoon over the lemon juice. Sprinkle with the lemon rind, chives, parsley, and salt and pepper to taste.
3. Wrap the foil loosely over the salmon and seal firmly with the join on top.
4. Place the parcels on a baking sheet and bake in the preheated oven for 20 minutes, or until the fish flakes easily.
5. Transfer the salmon and juices to warmed serving plates and serve immediately with salad and crusty bread.

TANDOORI SALMON

Serves: 2

Prep: 15 mins, plus marinating

Cook: 6–8 mins

Ingredients

2 salmon fillets, about 125 g/4½ oz each

oil, for brushing and greasing

sliced spring onion, to garnish

cooked basmati rice and cucumber raita, to serve

Spice mix

½ tsp ground coriander

½ tsp ground cumin

½ tsp cayenne pepper

½ tsp salt

½ tsp pepper

Method

1 Brush the salmon fillets lightly with a little oil. Combine the spice mix ingredients in a small bowl and rub generously into the salmon. Cover and leave to marinate in the refrigerator for 1 hour.

2 Preheat the grill to medium. Transfer the salmon to a sheet of lightly oiled foil and place on the grill pan. Cook under the preheated grill for 3–4 minutes on each side, or until cooked through.

3 Place the salmon on serving plates and sprinkle with the spring onions. Serve with basmati rice and cucumber raita.

SPICY TUNA FISH CAKES

Serves: 4 **Prep: 15–20 mins** **Cook: 8–10 mins**

Ingredients

- 200 g/7 oz canned tuna in oil, drained
- 2–3 tbsp curry paste
- 1 spring onion, finely chopped
- 1 egg, beaten
- 200 g/7 oz mashed potatoes
- 4 tbsp plain flour, plus extra for shaping
- sunflower oil or groundnut oil, for shallow-frying
- salt and pepper

Method

1. Place the tuna in a large mixing bowl. Add the curry paste, spring onion, egg and mashed potatoes. Season to taste with salt and pepper and mix together.
2. Divide the mixture into four portions and shape each into a ball. Then, on a floured surface, flatten slightly to make a patty shape of your preferred thickness. Season the flour to taste with salt and pepper. Dust each patty in the seasoned flour.
3. Heat the oil in a large frying pan, add the patties and fry for 3–4 minutes on each side, until crisp and golden. Serve immediately.

1
2

PAELLA

Serves: 4 **Prep: 15 mins** **Cook: 20 mins**

Ingredients

- 2 tbsp olive oil
- 1 onion, thinly sliced
- 1 red pepper, deseeded and sliced
- 100 g/3½ oz chorizo, sliced
- 200 g/7 oz long-grain rice
- 850 ml/1½ pints boiling fish stock
- pinch of saffron threads or ground turmeric
- 140 g/5 oz frozen peas
- 200 g/7 oz cooked, peeled large prawns
- salt and pepper
- chopped fresh flat-leaf parsley, to garnish

Method

1. Heat the oil in a large saucepan over a medium heat. Add the onion and red pepper and cook for 2 minutes, stirring constantly. Stir in the chorizo and rice and cook for a further 1 minute.
2. Add the stock and saffron and bring to the boil. Reduce the heat, cover the pan and simmer for 10 minutes, stirring occasionally, until the rice is almost tender.
3. Stir in the peas and prawns and season to taste with salt and pepper, then cover and cook gently for a further 4–5 minutes, until the rice is tender.
4. Transfer to warmed serving plates. Garnish with parsley and serve immediately.

1
1
2

RATATOUILLE

Serves: 4 **Prep: 15–20 mins** **Cook: 25–30 mins**

Ingredients

- 4 tbsp olive oil
- 1 onion, chopped
- 1 small aubergine, chopped
- 1 red pepper, deseeded and chopped
- 2 courgettes, chopped
- 2 garlic cloves, chopped
- 3 tbsp red wine
- 400 g/14 oz canned chopped tomatoes
- 2 bay leaves
- salt and pepper
- chopped fresh parsley, to garnish
- crusty bread, to serve

Method

1. Heat the oil in a large frying pan over a high heat. Add the onion and aubergine and cook for 5 minutes, until lightly browned. Add the red pepper and courgettes and cook, stirring, for a further 5 minutes, until the vegetables begin to soften.
2. Stir in the garlic, wine, tomatoes and bay leaves. Bring to the boil, then reduce the heat, cover and simmer for 10–15 minutes, stirring occasionally, until tender. Remove the bay leaves and season to taste with salt and pepper.
3. Transfer to warmed serving plates, garnish with parsley and serve immediately with crusty bread.

1
1
2

MUSHROOM STROGANOFF

Serves: 4 **Prep: 15 mins** **Cook: 15–20 mins**

Ingredients

25 g/1 oz butter
1 onion, finely chopped
450 g/1 lb closed-cup mushrooms, quartered
1 tsp tomato purée
1 tsp coarse grain mustard
150 ml/5 fl oz crème fraîche
1 tsp paprika, plus extra to garnish
salt and pepper
fresh flat-leaf parsley sprigs, to garnish

Method

1 Heat the butter in a large frying pan over a medium heat. Add the onion and cook gently for 5–10 minutes, until soft.

2 Add the mushrooms to the frying pan and stir-fry for a few minutes, until they begin to soften. Stir in the tomato purée and mustard, then add the crème fraîche and paprika. Cook gently, stirring constantly, for 5 minutes.

3 Season to taste with salt and pepper. Transfer to warmed serving plates and garnish with extra paprika and parsley sprigs. Serve immediately.

1
2
2

VEGETABLE TACOS

Serves: 4 **Prep: 15–20 mins** **Cook: 10–15 mins**

Ingredients

2 tbsp olive oil
1 red onion, sliced
2 small courgettes, diced
1 tsp ground coriander
½ tsp ground cumin
2 tomatoes, chopped
400 g/14 oz canned chickpeas, drained and rinsed
4 taco shells
85 g/3 oz Cheddar cheese, grated
salt and pepper

Method

1 Preheat the grill to high. Heat the oil in a large frying pan over a medium heat. Add the onion and courgettes and cook for 4–5 minutes, stirring occasionally.

2 Stir in the ground coriander and cumin, then add the tomatoes and chickpeas. Season to taste with salt and pepper and bring to the boil. Simmer over a medium heat, stirring occasionally, for 2 minutes. Spoon the mixture into the taco shells and sprinkle with the cheese.

3 Place on a baking sheet and cook the tacos under the preheated grill for 1–2 minutes, until the cheese has melted. Serve immediately.

2
2

CHILLI BEAN STEW

Serves: 4–6 **Prep: 20–25 mins** **Cook: 35–45 mins**

Ingredients

2 tbsp olive oil

1 onion, chopped

2–4 garlic cloves, chopped

2 fresh red chillies, deseeded and sliced

225 g/8 oz canned red kidney beans, drained and rinsed

225 g/8 oz canned cannellini beans, drained and rinsed

225 g/8 oz canned chickpeas, drained and rinsed

1 tbsp tomato purée

700–850 ml/1¼ –1½ pints vegetable stock

1 red pepper, deseeded and chopped

4 tomatoes, chopped

175 g/6 oz shelled fresh broad beans

1 tbsp chopped fresh coriander

paprika, to garnish

soured cream, to serve

Method

1 Heat the oil in a large, heavy-based saucepan with a tight-fitting lid. Add the onion, garlic and chillies and cook, stirring frequently, for 5 minutes, until soft.

2 Add the kidney beans, cannellini beans and chickpeas. Blend the tomato purée with a little of the stock and pour over the bean mixture, then add the remaining stock.

3 Bring to the boil, then reduce the heat and simmer for 10–15 minutes. Add the red pepper, tomatoes and broad beans.

4 Simmer for a further 15–20 minutes, or until all the vegetables are tender. Stir in most of the chopped coriander.

5 Garnish with the remaining chopped coriander and a pinch of paprika and serve topped with spoonfuls of soured cream.

2
3

4

BUTTERNUT SQUASH & MUSHROOM RISOTTO

Serves: 4 **Prep: 25 mins** **Cook: 50–55 mins**

Ingredients

2 tbsp olive oil

1 large onion, finely chopped

6 sage leaves, finely chopped

2 tsp chopped fresh thyme leaves

700 g/1 lb 9 oz butternut squash, peeled, deseeded and cut into 2-cm/ ¾-inch chunks

225 g/8 oz chestnut mushrooms, sliced

300 ml/10 fl oz vegetable stock

200 ml/7 fl oz dry white wine

350 g/12 oz risotto rice

55 g/2 oz freshly grated Parmesan cheese

salt and pepper

crispy fried sage leaves, to garnish

1 Preheat the oven to 200°C/400°F/Gas Mark 6. Heat the oil in a large saucepan. Add the onion, sage and thyme. Cover and cook over a low heat for 5 minutes, until the onion turns translucent.

2 Stir in the butternut squash, mushrooms, stock and wine. Bring to the boil, then remove from the heat and ladle everything in the pan into a large casserole. Stir in the rice.

3 Cover the casserole with a tight-fitting lid and bake in the preheated oven for 40–45 minutes, until the rice and vegetables are tender.

4 Stir in half the Parmesan, then season to taste with salt and pepper. Serve immediately sprinkled with the remaining Parmesan and garnished with fried sage leaves.

2
2

VEGETABLE BOLOGNESE

Serves: 2 **Prep: 15 mins** **Cook: 25 mins**

Ingredients

2 tbsp extra virgin olive oil
1 red onion, chopped
1 green pepper, deseeded and chopped
2 garlic cloves, chopped
1 tbsp tomato purée
400 g/14 oz canned chopped tomatoes
1 tsp sugar
85 g/3 oz mushrooms, sliced
125 ml/4 fl oz red wine or vegetable stock
200 g/7 oz dried tagliatelle
salt
freshly grated Parmesan cheese, to serve

Method

1. Heat the oil in a saucepan and cook the onion, green pepper and garlic for 3 minutes, or until softened. Stir in the tomato purée and cook for a further minute. Add the tomatoes, sugar, mushrooms and wine and bring to the boil. Cover and simmer for 15 minutes.
2. Meanwhile, bring a large saucepan of lightly salted water to the boil. Add the pasta, bring back to the boil and cook for 8–10 minutes, or until tender but still firm to the bite. Drain.
3. Serve the pasta with the bolognese sauce and grated Parmesan cheese.

HOME COMFORTS JUST LIKE MUM MAKES

SPAGHETTI WITH TUNA SAUCE

Serves: 4 **Prep: 15–20 mins** **Cook: 20 mins**

Ingredients

50 g/12 oz dried spaghetti

2 tbsp olive oil

1 garlic clove, peeled

1 onion, chopped

500 g/1 lb 2 oz tomatoes, chopped

400 g/14 oz canned tuna in spring water, drained and flaked

2 tbsp capers, rinsed (optional)

2 tbsp chopped fresh parsley, or 1 tbsp chopped fresh basil, or pinch of dried oregano

salt and pepper

Method

1 Bring a large saucepan of lightly salted water to the boil. Add the pasta, bring back to the boil and cook for 8–10 minutes, or until tender but still firm to the bite.

2 Meanwhile, heat the oil in a separate saucepan and add the garlic. When it has begun to colour, remove and discard it. Add the onion and tomatoes to the pan and cook over a low heat, stirring occasionally, for 5 minutes.

3 Drain the pasta and tip it into the pan with the onion and tomatoes. Add the tuna and capers, if using, and toss over the heat for a few minutes, until heated through. Remove from the heat. Season to taste with salt and pepper, stir in the herbs and serve immediately.

SPAGHETTI & MEATBALLS

Serves: 4

Prep: 30 mins, plus cooling

Cook: 40 mins

Ingredients

1 tbsp olive oil

1 small onion, finely chopped

2 garlic cloves, finely chopped

2 fresh thyme sprigs, leaves finely chopped

650 g/1 lb 7 oz fresh beef mince

25 g/1 oz fresh breadcrumbs

1 egg, lightly beaten

450 g/1 lb dried spaghetti

salt and pepper

Sauce

1 onion, cut into wedges

3 red peppers, halved and deseeded

400 g/14 oz canned chopped tomatoes

1 bay leaf

salt and pepper

Method

1 Preheat the grill. Put the onion wedges and pepper halves, skin-side up, on a grill rack and cook under the preheated grill, turning frequently, for 10 minutes, until the pepper skins are blistered and charred. Put the peppers into a plastic bag, tie the top and leave to cool. Set the onion wedges aside.

2 Meanwhile, heat the oil in a frying pan. Add the chopped onion and garlic and cook over a low heat, for 5 minutes, until softened. Tip the mixture into a bowl with the thyme, beef, breadcrumbs and egg. Season to taste with salt and pepper and mix well. Shape into 20 meatballs.

3 Heat a large, non-stick frying pan over a low–medium heat. Add the meatballs and cook, stirring gently and turning frequently, for 15 minutes, until lightly browned all over.

4 Peel off the pepper skins. Roughly chop the flesh and put it into a food processor or blender with the onion wedges and tomatoes. Process to a smooth purée and season to taste with salt and pepper. Pour into a saucepan with the bay leaf and bring to the boil. Reduce the heat and simmer, stirring occasionally, for 10 minutes. Remove and discard the bay leaf.

5 Meanwhile, bring a saucepan of lightly salted water to the boil. Add the spaghetti, bring back to the boil and cook for 8–10 minutes, until tender but still firm to the bite.

6 Drain the spaghetti and serve immediately with the meatballs and sauce.

SPAGHETTI CARBONARA

Serves: 4 **Prep: 20 mins** **Cook: 15 mins**

Ingredients

450 g/1 lb dried spaghetti
1 tbsp olive oil
225 g/8 oz rindless pancetta or streaky bacon, chopped
4 eggs
5 tbsp single cream
2 tbsp freshly grated Parmesan cheese
salt and pepper

Method

1 Bring a large, heavy-based saucepan of lightly salted water to the boil. Add the pasta, bring back to the boil and cook for 8–10 minutes, or until tender but still firm to the bite.

2 Meanwhile, heat the oil in a heavy-based frying pan. Add the pancetta and cook over a medium heat, stirring frequently, for 8–10 minutes.

3 Beat the eggs with the cream in a small bowl and season to taste with salt and pepper.

4 Drain the pasta and return it to the saucepan. Tip in the cooked pancetta, then add the egg mixture and half the Parmesan. Stir well, then transfer the spaghetti to a warmed serving dish.

5 Sprinkle with the remaining Parmesan and serve immediately.

CHEAT'S LASAGNE

Serves: 6

Prep: 20 mins,
plus standing

Cook: 1 hour 5 mins–
1¼ hours

Ingredients

- 2 tbsp olive oil
- 500 g/1 lb 2 oz fresh beef mince
- 1 onion, chopped
- 1 garlic clove, finely chopped
- 1 carrot, diced
- 1 tbsp chopped fresh flat-leaf parsley
- 6 fresh basil leaves, torn
- 600 ml/1 pint passata
- 550 g/1 lb 4 oz ricotta cheese
- 1 egg, lightly beaten
- 8 no pre-cook lasagne sheets
- 225 g/8 oz mozzarella cheese, grated
- salt and pepper

Method

1 Heat the oil in a saucepan. Add the beef, onion, garlic and carrot and cook over a medium heat, stirring frequently and breaking up the meat with a wooden spoon, for 5–8 minutes, until the beef is evenly browned.

2 Stir in the herbs, season to taste with salt and pepper and pour in the passata. Bring to the boil, then reduce the heat, cover and simmer for 15 minutes.

3 Meanwhile, preheat the oven to 190°C/375°F/Gas Mark 5. Mix the ricotta with the egg, stirring until smooth and thoroughly combined.

4 Make alternating layers of the beef mixture, lasagne sheets, ricotta mixture and mozzarella in an ovenproof dish, ending with a layer of mozzarella. Bake in the preheated oven for 40–45 minutes, until the topping is golden and bubbling. Leave to stand for 5 minutes before serving.

MACARONI CHEESE

Serves: 4 **Prep: 20 mins** **Cook: 30–40 mins**

Ingredients

250 g/9 oz dried macaroni

55 g/2 oz butter, plus extra for cooking the pasta

55 g/2 oz plain flour

600 ml/1 pint warm milk

200 g/7 oz Cheddar cheese, grated

55 g/2 oz freshly grated Parmesan cheese

½ tsp freshly grated nutmeg

salt and pepper

Method

1. Cook the pasta in a saucepan of lightly salted boiling water for 8–10 minutes, or until tender but still firm to the bite. Drain, then return to the pan with a small knob of butter and cover.
2. Meanwhile, melt the butter in a heavy-based saucepan over a low heat, then add the flour and stir to make a roux. Cook gently for 2 minutes. Add the milk a little at a time, whisking it into the roux, then cook for 10–15 minutes to make a loose, custard-style sauce.
3. Add three quarters of the Cheddar and all the Parmesan and stir through until melted. Season to taste with salt and pepper, add the nutmeg and remove from the heat.
4. Preheat the grill to high. Put the macaroni into a shallow, ovenproof dish, then pour the sauce over. Scatter over the remaining Cheddar and cook under the preheated grill until the cheese begins to brown. Serve immediately.

★ Variation

Stir 75 g/2¾ oz chopped ham and 200 g/7 oz canned, drained sweetcorn into the macaroni before pouring over the sauce.

DIY TAKEAWAYS

BLAZIN' BEEF TACOS

Serves: 2 **Prep: 20–25 mins** **Cook: 25–30 mins**

Ingredients

2 tbsp corn oil

1 small onion, finely chopped

2 garlic cloves, finely chopped

280 g/10 oz fresh beef mince

1½ tsp hot chilli powder

1 tsp ground cumin

8 taco shells

1 avocado

2 tbsp lemon juice

¼ head of lettuce, shredded

4 spring onions, thinly sliced

2 tomatoes, peeled and diced

125 ml/4 fl oz soured cream

115 g/4 oz Cheddar cheese, grated

salt and pepper

Method

1 Heat the oil in a frying pan. Add the onion and garlic and cook over a low heat, stirring occasionally, for 5 minutes, until softened. Add the beef, increase the heat to medium and cook, stirring frequently and breaking it up with a wooden spoon, for 8–10 minutes, until evenly browned. Drain off as much fat as possible.

2 Stir in the chilli powder and cumin, season to taste with salt and pepper and cook over a low heat, stirring frequently, for a further 8 minutes, then remove from the heat.

3 Heat the taco shells according to the packet instructions. Meanwhile, peel, stone and slice the avocado and gently toss with the lemon juice in a bowl.

4 Divide the lettuce, spring onions, tomatoes and avocado slices among the taco shells. Add a tablespoon of soured cream to each, then divide the beef mixture between them. Sprinkle with the cheese and serve immediately.

★ Variation

For a change, try using the same quantity of fresh chicken or turkey mince instead of the beef mince.

BURRITOS

Serves: 4 **Prep: 25–30 mins** **Cook: 1 hour–1 hour 10 mins**

Ingredients

1 tbsp olive oil

1 onion, chopped

1 garlic clove, finely chopped

500 g/1 lb 2 oz fresh lean beef mince

3 large tomatoes, deseeded and chopped

1 red pepper, deseeded and chopped

800 g/1 lb 12 oz canned mixed beans, drained and rinsed

125 ml/4 fl oz vegetable stock

1 tbsp finely chopped fresh parsley

8 wholemeal flour tortillas

125 ml/4 fl oz passata

50 g/1¾ oz Cheddar cheese, grated

3 spring onions, sliced

salt and pepper

Method

1 Heat the oil in a large, non-stick frying pan, add the onion and garlic and cook until the onion is soft but not brown. Remove from the pan.

2 Add the beef and cook over a high heat, breaking it up with a wooden spoon, until brown all over. Drain off as much fat as possible.

3 Return the onion and garlic to the pan, add the tomatoes and red pepper and cook for 8–10 minutes.

4 Add the beans, stock and parsley, season to taste with salt and pepper and cook, uncovered, for a further 20–30 minutes, until well thickened.

5 Meanwhile, preheat the oven to 180°C/350°F/Gas Mark 4. Mash the meat mixture to break up the beans, then divide between the tortillas. Roll up each tortilla and place seam-side down in a baking dish.

6 Pour the passata over the burritos and sprinkle over the cheese. Bake in the preheated oven for 20 minutes.

7 Remove from the oven and scatter over the spring onions. Serve immediately.

5
5

MUSHROOM FAJITAS

Serves: 4 **Prep: 15–20 mins** **Cook: 15–18 mins**

Ingredients

- 2 tbsp oil
- 500 g/1 lb 2 oz large flat mushrooms, sliced
- 1 onion, sliced
- 1 red pepper, deseeded and sliced
- 1 green pepper, deseeded and sliced
- 1 garlic clove, crushed
- ¼–½ tsp cayenne pepper
- juice and grated rind of 2 limes
- 2 tsp sugar
- 1 tsp dried oregano
- 8 flour tortillas
- salt and pepper
- salsa, to serve

Method

1. Heat the oil in a large frying pan over a medium heat. Add the mushrooms, onion, red pepper, green pepper and garlic and cook for 8–10 minutes, until the vegetables are cooked.
2. Add the cayenne pepper, lime juice and rind, sugar and oregano. Season to taste with salt and pepper and cook for a further 2 minutes. Remove the vegetables from the pan, set aside and keep warm.
3. Add the tortillas to a clean frying pan and warm for a few seconds on each side. Remove from the pan.
4. Divide the mushroom mixture between the tortillas. Roll up the tortillas and serve immediately with salsa.

2
4

GIANT MEAT FEAST PIZZA

Serves: 2

Prep: 35–40 mins, plus rising

Cook: 45 mins

Ingredients

Pizza base

400 g/14 oz strong bread flour, plus extra for dusting

1 tsp easy-blend dried yeast

1 tsp caster sugar

4 tbsp olive oil

1 tsp salt

250 ml/9 fl oz warm water

Meat sauce

2 tbsp olive oil

3 garlic cloves, sliced

100 g/3½ oz fresh lean beef mince

200 ml/7 fl oz passata

½ tsp dried oregano

100 ml/3½ fl oz water

salt and pepper

Topping

200 g/7 oz mozzarella cheese, torn

4 slices Parma ham

4 slices wafer-thin ham

40 g/1½ oz diced pancetta

100 g/3½ oz chorizo, sliced

40 g/1½ oz freshly grated Parmesan cheese

Method

1 In a large bowl, sift together the flour, yeast and caster sugar. Using a wooden spoon, slowly mix in the olive oil, salt and warm water. When a loose dough starts to form, tip out onto a floured surface and knead for 10 minutes, until smooth and elastic.

2 Put the dough in a clean bowl, cover with clingfilm and leave in a warm place for 1½ hours, or until the dough has doubled in size.

3 Meanwhile, place the oil and garlic in a saucepan and fry until the garlic starts to brown a little. Add the beef and cook for 10 minutes, until the it starts to brown. Add the passata, dried oregano and water and cook for 20 minutes, or until the sauce has reduced by half. Season to taste with salt and pepper and set aside.

4 Preheat the oven to 220°C/425°F/Gas Mark 7.

5 Once the dough has risen, knock back slightly and turn out onto a floured surface. Using a rolling pin, lightly roll the dough to fit a 30–38-cm/12–15-inch rectangular, non-stick baking sheet. Lay the dough on the baking sheet and push to the edges, if necessary.

6 Spread the meat sauce over the base of the pizza, leaving a 2.5-cm/1-inch border around the edges. Scatter over the mozzarella and then top with the rest of the meats and the Parmesan cheese.

7 Bake in the preheated oven for 10 minutes, or until golden and bubbling. Serve immediately.

VEGETABLE PIZZA

Serves: 1 **Prep: 15–20 mins** **Cook: 12–15 mins**

Ingredients

2 tbsp olive oil

30-cm/12-inch ready-made pizza base

3 tbsp tomato purée

1 onion, finely chopped

1 small green pepper, deseeded and thinly sliced

2 tomatoes, sliced

6 black olives, stoned and halved

100 g/3½ oz mozzarella cheese, torn into pieces

1 tbsp chopped fresh thyme

salt and pepper

Method

1. Preheat the oven to 220°C/425°F/Gas Mark 7. Brush a large baking sheet with a little of the oil and place the pizza base on the baking sheet.
2. Spread the tomato purée over the pizza base to within 2 cm/¾ inch of the edge. Arrange the onion, green pepper and tomatoes over the pizza.
3. Scatter over the olives and cheese. Sprinkle with the thyme and season to taste with salt and pepper, then drizzle with the remaining oil.
4. Bake in the preheated oven for 12–15 minutes, until bubbling and golden. Serve immediately.

2
2
3

MONSTER HOT DOGS

Serves: 2 **Prep: 15 mins** **Cook: 22 mins**

Ingredients

2 tbsp vegetable oil
2 large onions, sliced
4 large frankfurters
4 hot dog rolls

To serve

sliced dill pickles
American mustard
sweet pickle relish
grated Cheddar cheese

Method

1. In a medium-sized pan heat the oil over a medium heat and gently fry the onions for 20 minutes, or until soft and caramelized. Remove and set aside in a warm place.
2. Meanwhile, cook the frankfurters according to the packet instructions.
3. To serve, split the hot dog rolls and divide the frankfurters between them. Top with the onions, pickles, mustard, relish and cheese. Serve immediately.

QUICK & EASY CORN DOGS

Serves: 2 **Prep: 25 mins** **Cook: 35 mins**

Ingredients

oil, for deep-frying
100 g/3½ oz plain flour, sifted, plus 4 tbsp for dusting
300 g/10½ oz fine polenta
2 tbsp caster sugar
1 tsp smoked paprika
2 tsp mustard powder
1 tsp salt
1 tsp baking powder
2 large eggs
300 ml/10 fl oz buttermilk
150 ml/5 fl oz water
10 large frankfurters

Method

1 Heat enough oil for deep-frying in a saucepan or deep-fryer to 180–190°C/350–375°F, or until a cube of bread browns in 30 seconds.

2 Meanwhile, in a medium-sized bowl mix together the flour, polenta, sugar, paprika, mustard powder, salt and baking powder. Beat in the eggs using a wooden spoon then gradually add in the buttermilk and water and continue to beat until smooth and the consistency of double cream.

3 Insert a wooden skewer about three quarters of the way up each frankfurter. Place the remaining 4 tablespoons of flour in a bowl. Roll each frankfurter in the flour and then dip into the batter, turning to get an even coating and letting any excess batter drip off.

4 Lower the corn dogs into the hot oil in batches of two at a time and cook for 5 minutes, or until golden brown. Remove, drain on kitchen paper and keep warm. Repeat until all the corn dogs are cooked. Serve immediately.

CHILLI-FLAVOURED SPARE RIBS

Serves: 4

Prep: 20 mins, plus marinating

Cook: 1–1½ hours

Ingredients

1.8–2.25 kg/4–5 lb pork spare ribs

mashed potatoes and spring greens or cabbage, to serve

Smoky rub

2 tbsp mild chilli powder

2 tsp smoked paprika

2 tsp mild paprika

4 tsp dried oregano

2 tsp onion powder

2 tsp salt

Method

1. To make the smoky rub, combine the chilli powder, smoked paprika, mild paprika, oregano, onion powder and salt in a small bowl. Rub the mixture all over the ribs and set aside for 15 minutes to marinate.
2. Preheat the oven to 160°C/325°F/Gas Mark 3 and line a roasting tin with aluminium foil. Put a rack in the roasting tin. Place the ribs on the rack and roast for 1–1½ hours, or until cooked through and the meat is tender.
3. Remove the ribs from the oven and cut into serving portions. Serve with mashed potatoes and spring greens.

CHICKEN WINGS WITH HOT SAUCE

Serves: 2

Prep: 30 mins

Cook: 45–55 mins, plus resting

Ingredients

1.8 kg/4 lb chicken wings, thawed if frozen, patted dry

1 tbsp vegetable oil

1 tbsp plain flour

1 tsp salt

blue cheese dressing, to serve

Hot sauce

150 ml/5 fl oz hot red cayenne pepper sauce

115 g/4 oz cold unsalted-butter, cut into 2.5-cm/1-inch slices, plus extra for greasing

1½ tbsp white vinegar

¼ tsp Worcestershire sauce

1 tsp hot pepper sauce

¼ tsp cayenne pepper

pinch of garlic powder

salt and pepper

Method

1 Preheat the oven to 220°C/425°F/Gas Mark 7.

2 If using whole wings, cut each into two pieces. (The small wing tips can be discarded or saved for stock.) In a large mixing bowl, toss the wings with the oil, flour and salt until evenly coated.

3 Line two baking sheets with lightly greased foil. Divide the wings between the trays and spread them out evenly – do not overcrowd. Bake in the preheated oven for 25 minutes.

4 Meanwhile, mix all the sauce ingredients in a saucepan. Bring to a simmer, whisking, over a medium heat. Remove from the heat and set aside. Taste and adjust the seasoning, adding more salt and pepper if needed.

5 Remove the chicken wings from the oven, turn the wings over, then return them to the oven and cook for a further 20–30 minutes, depending on the size of the wings, until well browned and cooked through. Transfer to a large mixing bowl.

6 Pour the warm sauce over the hot wings and toss with a spoon or palette knife to completely coat. Leave to rest for 5 minutes. Before serving, toss again. Serve with blue cheese dressing.

COLOSSAL LAMB KEBABS WITH HOT CHILLI SAUCE

Serves: 2 **Prep: 20 mins** **Cook: 8–10 mins**

Ingredients

500 g/1 lb 2 oz leg of lamb, diced
2 tbsp olive oil
1 tsp dried thyme
1 tsp paprika
1 tsp ground cumin
2 large flatbreads
1 small red onion, sliced
1 tomato, chopped
small bunch of fresh coriander, chopped
juice of ½ lemon
salt and pepper
hot chilli sauce and natural yogurt, to serve

Method

1. In a medium-sized bowl mix the lamb with the oil, thyme and spices and season to taste with salt and pepper.
2. Preheat a large griddle pan or barbecue.
3. Thread the lamb onto two large skewers, and cook in the preheated pan for 4–5 minutes on each side, or until cooked to your liking.
4. Heat a large, dry frying pan and cook the flatbreads for a few seconds on both sides, until soft.
5. Remove the lamb from the skewers, divide between the flatbreads and top with the onion, tomato and coriander. Squeeze over the lemon juice and serve immediately, drizzled with chilli sauce and yogurt.

1
3
4

FALAFEL PITTA POCKETS

Serves: 4 **Prep: 30 mins** **Cook: 15–20 mins**

Ingredients

4 pitta breads
1 shallot, quartered
2–3 garlic cloves, peeled
425 g/15 oz canned chickpeas, drained and rinsed
30 g/1 oz fresh flat-leaf parsley leaves
1 tsp ground coriander
1 tsp ground cumin
½ tsp salt
⅛ tsp cayenne pepper
2 tbsp olive oil
2 tbsp plain flour
½ tsp baking powder
rapeseed oil, for frying
shredded lettuce, tomato slices, cucumber slices and Kalamata olives, to serve

Tahini dressing

2 tbsp tahini
juice of 1 lemon
2–3 tbsp water
½ tsp salt
⅛ tsp pepper
⅛ tsp cayenne pepper

Method

1. Preheat the oven to 200°C/400°F/Gas Mark 6. Wrap the pittas in aluminium foil and place in the preheated oven to warm through.
2. Place the shallot and garlic in a food processor and pulse a few times to chop. Add the chickpeas, parsley, ground coriander, cumin, salt, cayenne pepper, olive oil and flour. Process to a chunky purée. Add the baking powder and pulse once to incorporate.
3. To make the dressing, put all the ingredients in a small bowl and stir to combine.
4. Heat a depth of 5 mm/¼ inch of rapeseed oil in a large frying pan. Make walnut-sized balls out of the chickpea mixture, and then flatten the balls into 5 mm/¼ inch thick patties. When the oil is hot, add several patties to the pan and fry them for about 1½–2 minutes on each side, until well browned. Transfer to a plate lined with kitchen paper to drain. Repeat with the remaining patties until they have all been fried.
5. Remove the pittas from the oven and slice them in half. Stuff each half with 2–3 patties, drizzle with the dressing and fill with shredded lettuce, tomato slices and cucumber slices. Serve immediately with olives.

DOUBLE-DECKER BURGERS

Serves: 4 **Prep: 20 mins** **Cook: 10 mins**

Ingredients

900 g/2 lb fresh beef mince
2 tsp salt
½ tsp pepper
vegetable oil, for frying
8 Cheddar cheese slices
4 soft burger buns, split
lettuce leaves
tomato slices
red onion slices
gherkins, halved lengthways

Method

1. Place the beef in a medium-sized bowl with the salt and pepper and mix gently to combine. Divide into eight equal-sized portions and shape each portion into a patty no thicker than 1 cm/ ½ inch – the thinner the better for these burgers.
2. Place a large griddle pan over a medium–high heat. Add enough oil to coat the base of the pan. Add the patties and cook for about 4 minutes, without moving, until the burgers are brown and release easily from the pan. Turn and cook on the other side for 2 minutes, then put a slice of cheese on top of each burger and cook for a further 2 minutes, or until cooked to your liking.
3. Place a burger on each bun base, then place a second burger on top. Add the lettuce leaves, tomato slices, onion slices and gherkins. Finish with the bun tops and serve immediately.

AUSSIE BURGERS

Serves: 4 **Prep: 20 mins** **Cook: 15 mins**

Ingredients

450 g/1 lb fresh beef mince
2–3 tsp vegetable oil
4 slices canned pineapple rings, drained
4 eggs
4 tbsp mayonnaise
4 soft burger buns, split
4–8 slices beetroot in vinegar
lettuce leaves
tomato slices
salt and pepper

Method

1 Place the beef in a medium-sized bowl with 1 teaspoon salt and ½ teaspoon pepper. Mix gently to combine, then divide into four equal-sized portions and shape each portion into a patty.

2 Place a griddle pan over a medium-high heat and add 1 teaspoon of the oil. Lightly brush the pineapple with oil and place the patties and pineapple in the pan. Cover and cook the pineapple for 3 minutes on each side, until it is soft and marked, and cook the burgers for about 4 minutes on each side, until brown and cooked to your liking. Remove from the heat and keep warm.

3 Add enough of the remaining oil to a frying pan to lightly cover the base, swirling to coat the pan. Add the eggs and season to taste with salt and pepper. Cover and cook for about 3 minutes, until the whites are set and the yolks are beginning to set at the edges.

4 Spread some mayonnaise on each half of the buns. Place a pineapple slice on each bun base, then add a burger, egg, 1–2 beetroot slices, a lettuce leaf and tomato slices. Finish with the bun tops and serve immediately.

CHICKEN SLIDERS

Serves: 4 **Prep: 15–20 mins** **Cook: 8 mins**

Ingredients

4 chicken breast fillets (about 1 cm/½ inch thick)

225 ml/8 fl oz buttermilk

125 g/4½ oz plain flour

1 tbsp sweet paprika or smoked paprika

2 tsp garlic powder

1 tsp pepper

1 tsp salt

½ tsp cayenne pepper

125 ml/4 fl oz vegetable oil

4 tbsp mayonnaise

4 soft burger buns, split

tomato slices

lettuce leaves

coleslaw, to serve

Method

1 Place the chicken breasts in a bowl with the buttermilk and toss to coat.

2 Put the flour into a shallow bowl and add the paprika, garlic powder, pepper, salt and cayenne pepper. Stir to mix. Remove the chicken fillets, one at a time, from the buttermilk and dip them in the flour mixture. Return to the buttermilk and dip again in the flour mixture.

3 Heat the oil in a large frying pan over a medium–high heat until very hot. Add the chicken fillets in a single layer and cook for about 3 minutes on each side, until golden brown and cooked through.

4 Spread 1 tablespoon of the mayonnaise on the top half of each bun. Place tomato slices and lettuce leaves on the base of each bun. Top with a chicken fillet and finish with the burger tops. Serve immediately with coleslaw on the side.

BEAN BURGERS

Serves: 4 **Prep: 20–25 mins** **Cook: 20–25 mins**

Ingredients

1 tbsp sunflower oil, plus extra for brushing

1 onion, finely chopped

1 garlic clove, finely chopped

1 tsp ground coriander

1 tsp ground cumin

115 g/4 oz button mushrooms, finely chopped

425 g/15 oz canned red kidney beans, drained and rinsed

2 tbsp chopped fresh flat-leaf parsley

plain flour, for dusting

salt and pepper

4 soft burger buns, split

lettuce leaves, to serve

Method

1 Heat the oil in a heavy-based frying pan over a medium heat. Add the onion and cook, stirring frequently, for 5 minutes, or until soft.

2 Add the garlic, ground coriander and cumin and cook, stirring, for a further minute.

3 Add the mushrooms and cook, stirring frequently, for 4–5 minutes, until all the liquid has evaporated. Transfer to a bowl.

4 Put the beans into a bowl and mash with a potato masher. Stir into the mushroom mixture with the parsley and season to taste with salt and pepper.

5 Preheat the grill to medium–high. Divide the mixture into four equal-sized portions. Lightly dust with flour and shape into flat patties. Brush with oil and cook under the preheated grill for 4–5 minutes on each side.

6 Serve in the burger buns with the lettuce leaves.

CRISPY ONION RINGS

Serves: 4-6 **Prep: 25–30 mins** **Cook: 20–30 mins**

Ingredients

- 115 g/4 oz plain flour
- 1 egg
- 150 ml/5 fl oz semi-skimmed milk
- 4 large onions
- vegetable oil, for deep-frying
- chilli powder, to taste (optional)
- salt and pepper

Method

1 To make the batter, sift the flour and a pinch of salt into a large bowl and make a well in the centre. Break the egg into the well and gently beat with a whisk. Gradually whisk in the milk, drawing the flour from the side into the liquid in the centre to form a smooth batter.

2 Leaving the onions whole, slice widthways into 5-mm/¼-inch slices, then separate each slice into rings.

3 Heat enough oil for deep-frying in a large saucepan or deep-fryer to 180–190°C/350–375°F, or until a cube of bread browns in 30 seconds.

4 Using the tines of a fork, pick up several onions rings at a time and dip in the batter. Let any excess batter drip off, then add the onions to the oil and deep-fry for 1–2 minutes, until they rise to the surface of the oil and become crisp and golden brown. Remove from the oil, drain on kitchen paper and keep warm while deep-frying the remaining onion rings in batches. Do not try to deep-fry too many at a time, as this will reduce the temperature of the oil and the onion rings will become soggy.

5 Season the onion rings with chilli powder, if using, and salt and pepper to taste. Serve immediately.

CHEESY CHIPS

Serves: 4

Prep: 25 mins,
plus soaking & chilling

Cook: 35–50 mins

Ingredients

900 g/2 lb potatoes
vegetable oil, for deep-frying
sea salt

Cheese sauce

3 tbsp butter
3 tbsp plain flour
350 ml/12 fl oz milk
350 g/12 oz Cheddar cheese, grated
125 ml/4 fl oz soured cream
2 tsp Dijon mustard
½ tsp salt

Method

1 Cut the potatoes into 5 cm x 5-mm/2 inch x ¼-inch sticks. Soak the cut potatoes in a bowl of cold water for 5 minutes, then drain and rinse.

2 Cook the potatoes in a saucepan of lightly salted boiling water for 3–4 minutes, until they begin to soften. Drain the potatoes and spread on a baking sheet lined with kitchen paper. Chill for 1 hour or overnight.

3 To make the sauce, melt the butter in a saucepan over a medium heat. Whisk in the flour and cook for a further 30 seconds. Slowly add the milk and cook over a medium heat, whisking constantly, for a further 3 minutes, until the sauce thickens. Reduce the heat to low and add the cheese a little at a time, stirring after each addition until the cheese is completely melted. Stir in the soured cream, mustard and salt. Keep the sauce warm until ready to serve.

4 Heat enough oil for deep-frying in a large saucepan or a deep-fryer to 180–190°C/350–375°F, or until a cube of bread browns in 30 seconds. Carefully add the cut potatoes, in batches if necessary to avoid overcrowding. Cook for about 3–4 minutes, until beginning to brown. Remove using tongs and drain on a plate lined with kitchen paper.

5 Return the oil to 180–190°C/350–375°F, then add the potatoes again and fry for about 3–5 minutes, until golden brown and crisp. Remove from the oil and drain on a plate lined with kitchen paper. Season generously with sea salt.

6 Place the chips in a large bowl and serve the sauce in a bowl on the side for dipping. Alternatively, pour the sauce over the chips.

JUMBO POTATO WEDGES WITH DIPS

Serves: 4

Prep: 30 mins, plus cooling

Cook: 35 mins

Ingredients

6 large baking potatoes
6 tbsp olive oil
1 tbsp paprika
1 tsp dried oregano
small bunch of fresh thyme
3 garlic bulbs, tops cut off
4 tbsp mayonnaise
4 tbsp soured cream
2 tbsp creamed horseradish
small bunch of fresh chives, snipped
salt and pepper

Method

1. Preheat the oven to 200°C/400°F/Gas Mark 6.
2. Cut each potato in half lengthways, then cut each half into three wedges and place in a large bowl. Season to taste with salt and pepper and add the oil, paprika, oregano, thyme and garlic bulbs. Mix gently until all of the potatoes and garlic are covered.
3. Line a large baking sheet with baking paper and add the potatoes and garlic, making sure that you scrape everything out of the bowl. Cook in the preheated oven for 20 minutes, or until the garlic feels soft when pressed. Remove the garlic and set aside and turn the wedges over. Return the wedges to the oven and cook for a further 15 minutes. When the potatoes are cooked, remove from the oven and leave to cool for 5 minutes.
4. Meanwhile, put the mayonnaise and soured cream in separate bowls. Add the creamed horseradish and chives to the soured cream and mix well then set aside. Place the slightly cooled garlic bulbs on a clean surface and scrape out the cooked flesh with a knife, discarding the skin, then roughly chop and add to the mayonnaise.
5. Serve the potato wedges with the dips.

2
3
4

BEER-BATTERED FISH & CHIPS WITH MUSHY PEAS

Serves: 4 **Prep: 25 mins, plus chilling** **Cook: 45–50 mins**

Ingredients

225 g/8 oz self-raising flour, plus extra for dusting

300 ml/10 fl oz cold lager

vegetable oil, for deep-frying

6 large floury potatoes, such as King Edward, Maris Piper or Desirée, cut into chips

4 thick cod fillets, about 175 g/6 oz each

salt and pepper

lemon wedges, to serve

Mushy peas

350 g/12 oz frozen peas

30 g/1 oz butter

2 tbsp single cream

salt and pepper

Method

1 Sift the flour and ½ teaspoon salt into a large bowl, then whisk in most of the lager. Check the consistency of the batter and add the remaining lager if needed; it should be thick, like double cream. Chill in the refrigerator for 30 minutes.

2 Cook the peas in a saucepan of lightly salted boiling water for 3 minutes. Drain and mash to a thick purée, add the butter and cream and season with salt and pepper to taste. Set aside and keep warm.

3 Heat enough oil for deep-frying to 120°C/250°F in a deep-fryer or a large saucepan using a thermometer. Preheat the oven to 150°C/300°F/ Gas Mark 2.

4 Fry the potatoes for about 8–10 minutes, until softened but not coloured. Remove from the oil, drain on kitchen paper and place in a dish in the warm oven. Increase the temperature of the oil to 180°C/350°F.

5 Season the fish with salt and pepper to taste and dust lightly with a little flour. Dip one fillet in the batter and coat thickly. Carefully place in the hot oil and repeat with the other fillets (you may need to cook in batches). Cook for 8–10 minutes, turning them over halfway through. Remove the fish from the oil, drain and keep warm.

6 Reheat the oil to 180°C/350°F and cook the chips for a further 2–3 minutes, until golden brown. Drain and season with salt and pepper to taste. Serve the chips immediately with the fish, mushy peas and lemon wedges for squeezing over.

VEGETABLE KORMA

Serves: 4 **Prep: 20 mins** **Cook: 45 mins**

Ingredients

- 4 tbsp ghee or vegetable oil
- 2 onions, chopped
- 2 garlic cloves, chopped
- 1 fresh red chilli, chopped
- 1 tbsp grated fresh ginger
- 2 tomatoes, peeled and chopped
- 1 orange pepper, deseeded and cut into small pieces
- 1 large potato, cut into chunks
- 200 g/7 oz cauliflower florets
- ½ tsp salt
- 1 tsp ground turmeric
- 1 tsp ground cumin
- 1 tsp ground coriander
- 1 tsp garam masala
- 200 ml/7 fl oz vegetable stock or water
- 150 ml/5 fl oz natural yogurt
- 150 ml/5 fl oz single cream
- 25 g/1 oz fresh coriander, chopped

Method

1. Heat the ghee in a large saucepan over a medium heat. Add the onions and garlic and cook, stirring, for 3 minutes. Add the chilli and ginger and cook for a further 4 minutes.
2. Add the tomatoes, orange pepper, potato, cauliflower, salt and spices and cook, stirring, for a further 3 minutes. Stir in the stock and bring to the boil. Reduce the heat and simmer for 25 minutes.
3. Stir in the yogurt and cream. Reduce the heat and simmer gently, stirring, for a further 5 minutes. Add the chopped coriander and heat through. Serve immediately.

BEEF BALTI

Serves: 4 **Prep: 20 mins** **Cook: 25–30 mins**

Ingredients

- 2 tbsp ghee or vegetable oil
- 1 onion, thinly sliced
- 1 garlic clove, finely chopped
- 3-cm/1¼-inch piece fresh ginger, grated
- 2 fresh red chillies, deseeded and finely chopped
- 450 g/1 lb rump steak, cut into thin strips
- 1 green pepper, deseeded and thinly sliced
- 1 yellow pepper, deseeded and thinly sliced
- 1 tsp ground cumin
- 1 tbsp garam masala
- 4 tomatoes, chopped
- 2 tbsp lemon juice
- 1 tbsp water
- salt
- chopped fresh coriander, to garnish

Method

1. Heat 1 tablespoon of the ghee in a preheated wok or large, heavy-based frying pan. Add the onion and cook over a low heat, stirring occasionally, for 8–10 minutes, or until golden. Increase the heat to medium, add the garlic, ginger, chillies and steak and cook, stirring occasionally, for 5 minutes, or until the steak is browned all over. Remove with a slotted spoon, set aside and keep warm.
2. Add the remaining ghee to the wok. Add the peppers and cook over a medium heat, stirring occasionally, for 4 minutes, or until softened. Stir in the cumin and garam masala and cook, stirring, for 1 minute.
3. Add the tomatoes, lemon juice and water, season to taste with salt and simmer, stirring constantly, for 3 minutes. Return the steak mixture to the wok and heat through. Transfer to a warmed serving dish, garnish with coriander and serve immediately.

THAI GREEN CHICKEN CURRY

Serves: 4 **Prep: 15 mins** **Cook: 15–20 mins**

Ingredients

2 tbsp groundnut oil or vegetable oil

4 spring onions, roughly chopped

2 tbsp Thai green curry paste

700 ml/1¼ pints canned coconut milk

1 chicken stock cube

6 skinless, boneless chicken breasts, about 115 g/4 oz each, cut into 2.5-cm/1-inch cubes

large handful of fresh coriander, chopped

1 tsp salt

cooked rice, to serve

Method

1. Heat the oil in a preheated wok, add the spring onions and stir-fry over a medium–high heat for 30 seconds, or until starting to soften.
2. Add the curry paste, coconut milk and stock cube. Bring gently to the boil, stirring occasionally.
3. Add the chicken, half the coriander and the salt and stir well. Reduce the heat and simmer gently for 8–10 minutes, until the chicken is cooked through and tender.
4. Stir in the remaining coriander. Serve immediately with cooked rice.

SLICED BEEF IN BLACK BEAN SAUCE

Serves: 4 **Prep: 15 mins** **Cook: 10–12 mins**

Ingredients

3 tbsp groundnut oil

450 g/1 lb sirloin steak, thinly sliced

1 red pepper, deseeded and thinly sliced

1 green pepper, deseeded and thinly sliced

1 bunch of spring onions, sliced

2 garlic cloves, crushed

1 tbsp grated fresh ginger

2 tbsp black bean sauce

1 tbsp sherry

1 tbsp soy sauce

Method

1 Preheat a wok or large frying pan over a high heat. Add 2 tablespoons of the oil and heat until very hot. Add the beef and stir-fry until starting to brown. Remove and set aside.

2 Add the remaining oil and the peppers and stir-fry for 2 minutes.

3 Add the spring onions, garlic and ginger and stir-fry for 30 seconds.

4 Add the black bean sauce, sherry and soy sauce, then stir in the beef and heat until bubbling. Serve immediately.

CHICKEN CHOW MEIN

Serves: 2 **Prep: 15 mins** **Cook: 15–18 mins**

Ingredients

100g/3½ oz wholewheat ribbon noodles

2 tbsp sesame oil or vegetable oil

300 g/10½ oz skinless, boneless chicken breasts, cut into strips

1 courgette, thinly sliced

1 carrot, thinly sliced

1 red pepper, deseeded and thinly sliced

50 g/1¾ oz mangetout or sugar snap peas

4 large spring onions, thinly sliced

2 tsp Chinese five-spice

1 tbsp light soy sauce

1 tbsp oyster sauce

3–4 tbsp chicken stock

Method

1. Cook the noodles in a saucepan of boiling water for 2–3 minutes, or according to the packet instructions, until just tender but still with some bite.
2. Heat the oil in a wok or non-stick frying pan and stir-fry the chicken with the courgette, carrot, red pepper, mangetout and spring onions over a high heat for 5 minutes, until the chicken is cooked through and the vegetables are tender.
3. Add the Chinese five-spice, soy sauce, oyster sauce and stock and stir for a further minute. Drain the noodles, add to the pan and stir again for 1 minute before serving.

SWEET & SOUR PORK

Serves: 4 **Prep: 15 mins** **Cook: 10–12 mins**

Ingredients

1 tbsp vegetable oil

350 g/12 oz lean pork, cut into 5-mm/¼-inch strips

1 large red pepper, deseeded and sliced

4 spring onions, chopped, plus extra shredded spring onions to garnish

450 g/1 lb canned pineapple pieces in juice

2 tbsp cornflour

3 tbsp wine vinegar

juice of 1 lemon

3 tbsp light soy sauce

2 tbsp granulated sugar

salt and pepper

Method

1 Heat the oil in a wok or large frying pan, add the pork strips and cook for 5 minutes, stirring.

2 Add the red pepper and chopped spring onions to the wok and cook, stirring, for 3 minutes, until they begin to soften.

3 Drain the pineapple juice into a bowl, reserving the pineapple pieces, and whisk in the cornflour, vinegar, lemon juice, soy sauce, sugar, and salt and pepper to taste.

4 Add the mixture to the wok and cook over a medium heat for 1–2 minutes, stirring, until slightly thickened. Add the reserved pineapple pieces and heat through for 1 minute. Garnish with shredded spring onions and serve immediately.

PAD THAI

Serves: 4 **Prep: 20–25 mins** **Cook: 8–12 mins**

Ingredients

- 225 g/8 oz thick rice noodles
- 2 tbsp groundnut or vegetable oil
- 4 spring onions, roughly chopped, plus extra to garnish
- 2 garlic cloves, crushed
- 2 fresh red chillies, deseeded and sliced
- 225 g/8 oz pork fillet, trimmed and thinly sliced
- 115 g/4 oz cooked, peeled large prawns
- juice of 1 lime
- 2 tbsp Thai fish sauce
- 2 eggs, beaten
- 55 g/2 oz fresh beansprouts
- handful of chopped fresh coriander
- 55 g/2 oz unsalted peanuts, chopped

Method

1 Prepare the noodles according to the packet instructions. Drain and set aside.

2 Heat a wok or large frying pan over a medium–high heat, then add the oil. Add the spring onions, garlic and chillies and stir-fry for 1–2 minutes. Add the pork and stir-fry over a high heat for 1–2 minutes, until cooked through.

3 Add the prawns, lime juice, fish sauce and eggs and stir-fry over a medium heat for 2–3 minutes, until the eggs have set and the prawns are heated through.

4 Add the beansprouts, coriander, peanuts and noodles and stir-fry for 30 seconds, until heated through. Garnish with spring onions and serve immediately.

2
3
4

SATAY NOODLES

Serves: 2 **Prep: 15 mins** **Cook: 15–18 mins**

Ingredients

- 125 g/4½ oz medium egg noodles
- 150 ml/5 fl oz boiling water
- 85 g/3 oz creamed coconut, chopped
- 2 tsp oil
- 1 large red pepper, deseeded and thinly sliced
- 1 large garlic clove, thinly sliced
- 125 g/4½ oz fresh beansprouts
- 2 tbsp dark soy sauce
- 55 g/2 oz roasted salted peanuts, roughly chopped
- 3 spring onions, diagonally sliced
- large handful of fresh coriander leaves, chopped
- salt

Method

1. Bring a large saucepan of lightly salted water to the boil. Add the noodles, bring back to the boil and cook for 4 minutes, or until tender but still firm to the bite. Drain.
2. Place the boiling water in a small bowl and stir in the creamed coconut until dissolved. Set aside.
3. Heat the oil in a wok or a large frying pan. Add the red pepper and stir-fry over a high heat for 2–3 minutes, until soft. Add the garlic and stir-fry for a further 40–60 seconds, taking care that it doesn't burn.
4. Add the beansprouts to the wok, followed by the noodles, dissolved coconut, soy sauce and peanuts. Reduce the heat and stir for a further 2–3 minutes, until piping hot. Add the spring onions and coriander and toss together. Serve immediately.

2
3
4

CHINESE VEGETABLE RICE

Serves: 4 **Prep: 20 mins** **Cook: 25 mins**

Ingredients

- 350 g/12 oz long-grain rice
- 1 tsp ground turmeric
- 2 tbsp sunflower oil
- 225 g/8 oz courgettes, sliced
- 1 red pepper, deseeded and sliced
- 1 green pepper, deseeded and sliced
- 1 fresh green chilli, deseeded and finely chopped
- 1 carrot, coarsely grated
- 150 g/5½ oz fresh beansprouts
- 6 spring onions, sliced
- 2 tbsp soy sauce
- salt
- fresh coriander leaves, to garnish (optional)

Method

1. Place the rice and turmeric in a saucepan of lightly salted water and bring to the boil. Reduce the heat and leave to simmer for 8–10 minutes, or until the rice is just tender. Drain the rice thoroughly and press out any excess water with a sheet of kitchen paper. Set aside.
2. Heat the wok or large frying pan over a medium–high heat, then add the oil. Add the courgettes to the wok and stir-fry for about 2 minutes. Add the peppers and chilli and stir-fry for 2–3 minutes.
3. Stir the cooked rice into the wok, a little at a time, tossing well after each addition. Add the carrot, beansprouts and spring onions to the wok and stir-fry for a further 2 minutes.
4. Drizzle over the soy sauce and stir well. Transfer to serving bowls and scatter over the coriander leaves, if using. Serve immediately.

★ Variation

For a tasty topping, heat 1 teaspoon sunflower oil in a small non-stick frying pan and add 2 beaten eggs. Cook as an omelette until set, then remove from the pan and cut into slivers.

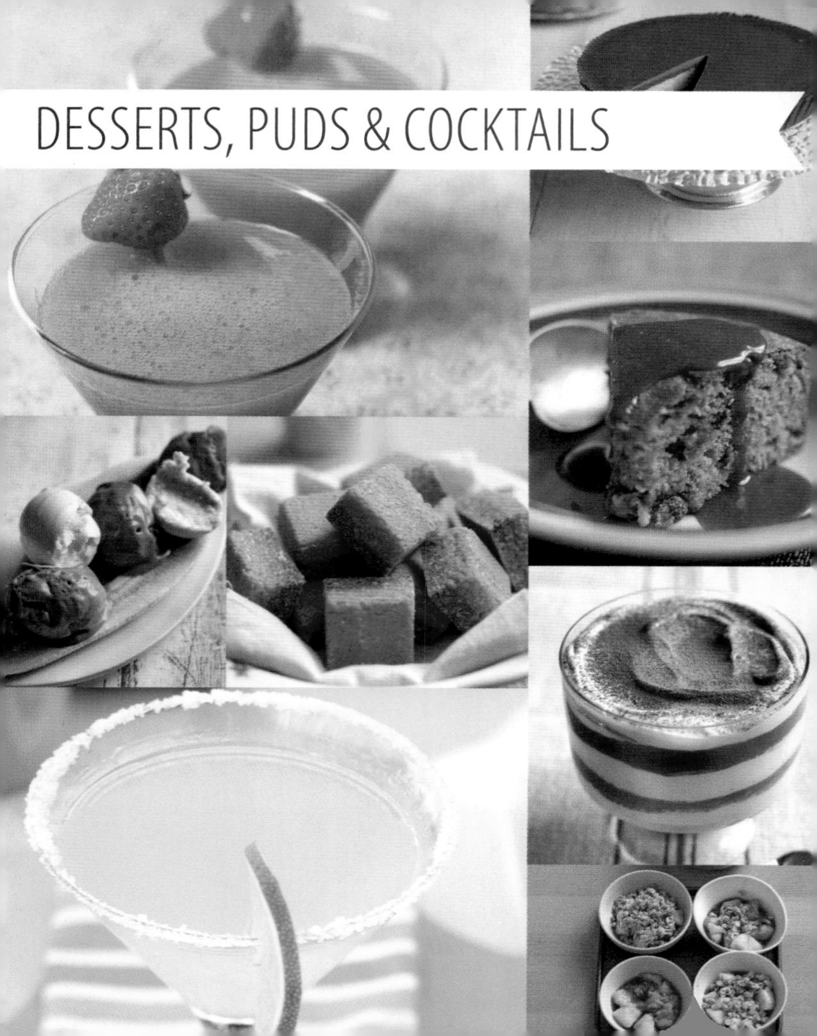

DESSERTS, PUDS & COCKTAILS

BEERAMISU

Serves: 8

Prep: 20–25 mins, plus chilling

Cook: N/A

Ingredients

750 g/1 lb 10 oz mascarpone cheese
600 ml/1 pint double cream
300 g/10½ oz caster sugar
450 ml/16 fl oz stout
1 tbsp vanilla extract
50 sponge fingers
2 double shots espresso
400 ml/14 fl oz Irish cream liqueur
cocoa powder, for dusting

Method

1 In a large bowl beat together the mascarpone cheese, cream and sugar until combined. Gradually add the stout and vanilla extract and beat until the mixture resembles a thick cream.

2 In a medium-sized bowl soak the sponge fingers in the espresso and Irish cream liqueur for around 10 seconds, and then break up the softened biscuits using a spoon.

3 In a 4-litre/7-pint dish or bowl layer the mascarpone mixture and then the soaked biscuit mixture alternately until there are two layers of each mixture. Finish off with one more layer of the mascarpone mixture.

4 Chill in the refrigerator for at least 3 hours, or until needed. To serve, remove from the refrigerator and dust with cocoa powder.

★ Variation

For a more traditional take on tiramisu, replace the stout with Marsala and the Irish cream liqueur with extra espresso or a mixture of espresso and almond liqueur.

CHOCOLATE PUDDING

Serves: 6 **Prep: 15 mins** **Cook: 12–15 mins**

Ingredients

100 g/3½ oz sugar
4 tbsp cocoa powder
2 tbsp cornflour
pinch of salt
350 ml/12 fl oz milk
1 egg, beaten
55 g/2 oz butter
½ tsp vanilla extract
double cream, to serve

Method

1 Mix together the sugar, cocoa powder, cornflour and salt in a heatproof bowl and set aside.

2 Pour the milk into a saucepan and heat over a medium heat until just simmering. Do not bring to a boil.

3 Keeping the pan over a medium heat, spoon a little of the simmering milk into the sugar mixture and blend, then stir this mixture into the milk in the pan. Beat in the egg and half the butter and reduce the heat to low.

4 Simmer for 5–8 minutes, stirring frequently, until the mixture thickens. Remove from the heat and add the vanilla extract and the remaining butter, stirring until the butter melts.

5 Transfer to serving bowls. Drizzle with double cream and serve immediately.

1
2
3

ETON MESS

Serves: 4–6

Prep: 35–40 mins, plus cooling

Cook: 45–50 mins

Ingredients

- 3 egg whites
- 175 g/6 oz caster sugar
- 700 g/1 lb 9 oz strawberries, hulled
- 2 tbsp icing sugar
- 2 tbsp crème de fraise (strawberry liqueur) (optional)
- 300 ml/10 fl oz double cream
- 150 ml/5 fl oz single cream

Method

1. Preheat the oven to 150°C/300°F/Gas Mark 2.
2. Whisk the egg whites in a mixing bowl until thick and forming soft peaks. Add the sugar gradually, whisking well after each addition. The meringue mixture should be glossy and firm.
3. Spoon the meringue onto a baking sheet lined with baking paper and spread into a rough 30-cm/12-inch round. Cook in the preheated oven for 45–50 minutes, until the meringue is firm on the outside but still soft in the centre. Remove from the oven and allow to cool.
4. Place a third of the strawberries (choose the larger ones) in a blender or food processor and purée with the icing sugar. Pour the purée into a bowl, add the liqueur, if using, and the remaining strawberries and stir until well mixed.
5. Whip together the double and single cream until thick but still light and floppy.
6. Break the meringue into large pieces and place half in a large bowl. Spoon over half the fruit mixture and half the cream. Layer up the remaining ingredients and lightly fold the mixture together so you have a streaky appearance. Serve immediately after mixing or the meringues will soften.

STICKY TOFFEE PUDDING

Serves: 8

Prep: 20–25 mins, plus soaking

Cook: 40–45 mins

Ingredients

75 g/2¾ oz sultanas

150 g/5½ oz stoned dates, chopped

1 tsp bicarbonate of soda

25 g/1 oz butter, plus extra for greasing

200 g/7 oz soft light brown sugar

2 eggs

200 g/7 oz self-raising flour, sifted

Sticky toffee sauce

25 g/1 oz butter

175 ml/6 fl oz double cream

200 g/7 oz soft light brown sugar

Method

1 Preheat the oven to 180°C/350°F/Gas Mark 4. Grease a 20-cm/8-inch round cake tin.

2 Put the sultanas, dates and bicarbonate of soda into a heatproof bowl. Cover with boiling water and leave to soak.

3 Put the butter into a separate bowl, add the sugar and mix well. Beat the eggs into the butter mixture, then fold in the flour. Drain the soaked fruit, add to the bowl and mix.

4 Spoon the mixture evenly into the prepared tin. Bake in the preheated oven for 35–40 minutes, or until a skewer inserted into the centre comes out clean.

5 About 5 minutes before the end of the cooking time, make the sauce. Melt the butter in a saucepan over a medium heat. Stir in the cream and sugar and bring to the boil, stirring constantly. Reduce the heat and simmer for 5 minutes.

6 Cut the pudding into wedges, pour over the sauce and serve immediately.

2
3
3

JAM ROLY-POLY

Serves: 6

Prep: 30 mins,
plus resting & cooling

Cook: 1 hour 35 mins–
2 hours 5 mins

Ingredients

225 g/8 oz self-raising flour, plus extra for dusting

pinch of salt

115 g/4 oz suet

grated rind of 1 lemon

1 tbsp sugar

50 ml/2 fl oz milk, plus 2 tbsp for brushing

50 ml/2 fl oz water

4–6 tbsp strawberry jam

ready-made custard, to serve

Method

1 Sift the flour into a mixing bowl and add the salt and suet. Mix together well. Stir in the lemon rind and sugar.

2 Mix together the milk and the water in a jug. Make a well in the centre of the dry ingredients and add the liquid ingredients to give a light, elastic dough. Knead lightly until smooth. If you have time, wrap the dough in clingfilm and leave it to rest for 30 minutes.

3 On a lightly floured surface, roll out the dough into a 20 x 25-cm/8 x 10-inch rectangle.

4 Spread the jam over the dough, leaving a 1-cm/½-inch border. Brush the border with the milk and roll up the dough carefully, like a Swiss roll, from one short end. Seal the ends. Wrap the roly-poly loosely in greaseproof paper and then in foil, sealing the ends well.

5 Prepare a steamer by half filling it with water and putting it on to boil. Place the roly-poly in the steamer and steam over rapidly boiling water for 1½–2 hours, making sure you top up the water from time to time.

6 When cooked, remove from the steamer and leave to cool slightly. Unwrap, cut into slices and serve immediately with the custard.

1
3
4

TREACLE TART

Serves: 8

Prep: 30 mins,
plus chilling & cooling

Cook: 35–40 mins

Ingredients

- 250 g/9 oz ready-made shortcrust pastry
- plain flour, for dusting
- 350 g/12 oz golden syrup
- 125 g/4½ oz fresh white breadcrumbs
- 125 ml/4 fl oz double cream
- finely grated rind of ½ lemon or orange
- 2 tbsp lemon juice or orange juice
- whipped cream, to serve

Method

1. Roll out the pastry on a lightly floured work surface and use to line a 20-cm/8-inch tart tin, reserving the pastry trimmings. Prick the base of the pastry case all over with a fork, cover with clingfilm and chill in the refrigerator for 30 minutes. Re-roll the reserved pastry trimmings and cut out small shapes, such as leaves, stars or hearts, to decorate the top of the tart.
2. Preheat the oven to 190°C/375°F/Gas Mark 5. Mix the golden syrup, breadcrumbs, double cream and lemon rind with the lemon juice in a small bowl.
3. Pour the mixture into the pastry case and decorate the top of the tart with the pastry shapes of your choice. Transfer to the preheated oven and bake for 35–40 minutes, or until the filling is just set.
4. Leave the tart to cool slightly before serving. Cut into wedges and serve with cream.

SYRUP SPONGE

Serves: 4 **Prep: 20 mins** **Cook: 4 mins, plus standing**

Ingredients

- 4 tbsp golden syrup
- 125 g/4½ oz butter, plus extra for greasing
- 85 g/3 oz caster sugar
- 2 eggs, lightly beaten
- 125 g/4½ oz self-raising flour
- 1 tsp baking powder
- about 2 tbsp warm water
- ready-made custard, to serve

Method

1. Grease a 1.5-litre/2¾-pint pudding basin or microwave-safe bowl with butter. Spoon the golden syrup into the prepared basin.
2. Beat the butter with the sugar in a bowl until pale and fluffy. Gradually add the eggs, beating well after each addition.
3. Sift together the flour and baking powder, then gently fold into the butter mixture. Add enough of the warm water to give a soft, dropping consistency. Spoon the mixture into the basin and level the surface.
4. Cover with microwave-safe clingfilm, leaving a small space to let the air escape. Cook in a microwave oven on high for 4 minutes, then remove and leave the pudding to stand for 5 minutes while it continues to cook.
5. Turn the pudding out onto a serving plate. Cut into wedges and serve with custard.

MINI APPLE CRUMBLES

Serves: 4 **Prep: 15 mins** **Cook: 20 mins**

Ingredients

- 2 large Bramley apples, peeled, cored and chopped
- 3 tbsp maple syrup
- juice of ½ lemon
- ½ tsp ground allspice
- 55 g/2 oz unsalted butter
- 100 g/3½ oz rolled oats
- 40 g/1½ oz light muscovado sugar

Method

1. Preheat the oven to 220°C/425°F/Gas Mark 7. Place a baking sheet in the oven to heat. Put the apples into a saucepan and stir in the maple syrup, lemon juice and allspice.
2. Bring to the boil over a high heat, then reduce the heat to medium, cover the pan and cook for 5 minutes, or until almost tender.
3. Meanwhile, melt the butter in a separate saucepan, then remove from the heat and stir in the oats and sugar.
4. Divide the apples between four 200-ml/7-fl oz ovenproof dishes. Sprinkle over the oat mixture. Place on the baking sheet in the preheated oven and bake for 10 minutes, until lightly browned and bubbling. Serve warm.

3
4

BIG BANANA SPLIT

Serves: 1 **Prep: 15 mins** **Cook: N/A**

Ingredients

1 large banana

500 ml/18 fl oz chocolate ice cream

250 ml/9 fl oz clotted cream

100 ml/3½ fl oz caramel sauce

55 g/2 oz pecan nuts, crushed

55 g/2 oz maraschino cherries

Method

1. Peel and split the banana lengthways, then put onto an oblong serving plate.
2. Put three large scoops of chocolate ice cream on top, then add three scoops of clotted cream.
3. Drizzle over the caramel sauce, top with the crushed nuts and cherries and serve immediately.

1
2
3

COOKIE DOUGH ICE CREAM

Serves: 8

Prep: 25–30 mins, plus chilling, cooling & freezing

Cook: 10 mins

Ingredients

Cookie dough

- 100 g/3½ oz butter, softened
- 55 g/2 oz soft light brown sugar
- 55 g/2 oz soft dark brown sugar
- 1½ tsp vanilla extract
- 175 g/6 oz plain flour
- 100 g/3½ oz dark chocolate chips

Ice cream

- 450 ml/16 fl oz whole milk
- 12 egg yolks
- 1½ tsp vanilla extract
- 300 g/10½ oz caster sugar
- 450 ml/16 fl oz double cream

Method

1. In a food processor beat together the butter, light brown sugar and dark brown sugar until pale and fluffy. Add the vanilla extract and all the flour, then pulse the mixture until it starts to come together. Turn the mixture onto a clean surface and fold in the chocolate chips by hand. Wrap in clingfilm and chill in the refrigerator for 30 minutes.
2. Meanwhile, slowly heat the milk in a heavy-based pan.
3. In a medium-sized heatproof bowl, whisk together the egg yolks, vanilla extract and the caster sugar.
4. When the milk comes to the boil, remove from the heat and gradually pour it into the egg mixture, whisking as you pour. Then pour the mixture back into a clean pan, stir with a wooden spoon and slowly heat until the sauce thickens, taking care that the mixture does not boil. Add the double cream and leave to cool slightly.
5. Freeze the mixture in a freezerproof container, uncovered, for 1–2 hours, until beginning to set around the edges.
6. Meanwhile, remove the cookie dough from the refrigerator and break into walnut-sized pieces.

7 Turn the ice cream out into a bowl and stir with a fork until smooth. Stir in the dough pieces, then return to the freezerproof container and freeze for a further 2–3 hours, or until set. Alternatively, use an ice-cream machine to churn the ice cream following the manufacturer's instructions, taking care not to break up the dough pieces too much.

PIÑA COLADA LOLLIES

Makes: 8

Prep: 25 mins, plus freezing

Cook: N/A

Ingredients

600 g/1 lb 5 oz pineapple flesh, finely diced

200 ml/7 fl oz coconut milk

6 tbsp caster sugar

2 tbsp coconut-flavoured white rum

Method

1 Drop a tablespoon of the diced pineapple into each of eight 100-ml/3½-fl oz ice lolly moulds.

2 Put the remaining pineapple in a blender with the coconut milk, sugar and rum and whizz until smooth.

3 Sieve using a fine metal sieve, pressing down to extract all the juice. Discard the solids. Pour the mixture into the ice lolly moulds. Insert the ice lolly sticks and freeze for 6–8 hours, or until firm.

4 To unmould the ice lollies, dip the frozen moulds into warm water for a few seconds and gently release the lollies while holding the sticks.

PEANUT BUTTER S'MORES

Makes: 3

Prep: 10 mins,
plus cooling

Cook: 1 mins

Ingredients

115 g/4 oz smooth peanut butter

6 graham crackers or digestive biscuits

85 g/3 oz plain chocolate, broken into squares

Method

1 Preheat the grill to high. Spread the peanut butter on one side of each cracker.

2 Place the chocolate pieces on three of the crackers and invert the remaining crackers on top.

3 Toast the s'mores under the preheated grill for about 1 minute, until the filling starts to melt. Turn carefully using tongs. Leave to cool slightly, then serve.

ROCKY ROAD BARS

Makes: 8

Prep: 20 mins, plus cooling & chilling

Cook: 5 mins

Ingredients

175 g/6 oz milk or plain chocolate

55 g/2 oz butter

100 g/3½ oz shortcake biscuits, broken into pieces

85 g/3 oz white mini marshmallows

85 g/3 oz walnuts or peanuts

icing sugar, sifted, for dusting

Method

1. Line an 18-cm/7-inch square cake tin with baking paper.
2. Break the chocolate into squares and place in a heatproof bowl. Set the bowl over a saucepan of gently simmering water and heat until the chocolate is melted, taking care that the bowl does not touch the water.
3. Add the butter and stir until melted and combined. Leave to cool slightly.
4. Stir the broken biscuits, marshmallows and nuts into the chocolate mixture.
5. Pour the chocolate mixture into the lined tin, pressing down with the back of a spoon. Chill in the refrigerator for at least 2 hours, or until firm.
6. Carefully turn out of the tin onto a wooden board. Dust with icing sugar and cut into bars.

PARTY-SIZED POPCORN BALL

Serves: 2–3 **Prep: 10–12 mins, plus cooling** **Cook: 15 mins**

Ingredients

1 tbsp sunflower oil
55 g/2 oz popping corn
225 g/8 oz sugar
2 tbsp golden syrup
150 ml/5 fl oz water
butter, for greasing

Method

1 Line a baking sheet with baking paper and set aside. Heat the oil in a large, deep saucepan with a lid. Add the corn, cover the pan and cook over a high heat, shaking the pan frequently, until all the corn has popped. Transfer to a large, heatproof bowl, discarding any un-popped corn.

2 Put the sugar, golden syrup and water into a large, heavy-based saucepan and heat gently, stirring constantly, until the sugar has dissolved. Increase the heat and boil for 5–6 minutes, without stirring, until a golden caramel has formed.

3 Quickly pour the caramel over the popcorn and mix well. When the popcorn is just cool enough to handle, use buttered hands to shape into a large ball. Place on the prepared baking sheet and leave to cool.

COCONUT ICE

Makes: 50

Prep: 25 mins, plus setting

Cook: N/A

Ingredients

oil, for greasing

400 g/14 oz canned condensed milk

1 tsp vanilla extract

300 g/10½ oz desiccated coconut

300 g/10½ oz icing sugar

3 tbsp cocoa powder, sifted

few drops of red or pink food colouring (optional)

Method

1 Grease the base of a shallow 18-cm/7-inch square cake tin and line with baking paper. Mix together the condensed milk and vanilla extract in a large bowl. Add the coconut and icing sugar. Stir with a wooden spoon until the mixture becomes very stiff.

2 Transfer half of the mixture to another bowl. Add the cocoa powder and mix well until it is an even colour. Spread over the base of the prepared tin and press down with the back of a spoon.

3 If using food colouring, mix a few drops into the remaining bowl of mixture until evenly pink in colour. Spread over the chocolate layer and smooth the top. Leave to set overnight before turning out and cutting into squares.

GIANT PEANUT BUTTER CUP

Serves: 12

Prep: 25–30 mins, plus cooling, chilling & standing

Cook: 15–20 mins

Ingredients

225 g/8 oz smooth peanut butter

115 g/4 oz soft light brown sugar

1 tsp vanilla extract

85 g/3 oz butter

115 g/4 oz icing sugar

350 g/12 oz milk chocolate, broken into pieces

350 g/12 oz plain chocolate, broken into pieces

Method

1 To make the filling, put the peanut butter, brown sugar, vanilla extract and half the butter into a saucepan and heat gently until the butter has melted and the sugar has dissolved, stirring constantly. Simmer for 2–3 minutes, then remove from the heat and gradually beat in the icing sugar. Transfer to a bowl and leave to cool.

2 Put the milk chocolate, plain chocolate and the remaining butter into a large, heatproof bowl set over a saucepan of barely simmering water and leave until melted, stirring occasionally. Take care that the base of the bowl does not touch the water. Remove from the heat and stir until smooth.

3 Place two 20-cm/8-inch round, non-stick cake liners in a double layer in a 23-cm/9-inch tart tin (this keeps the shape of the peanut butter cup and makes it easier to transfer to the refrigerator). Pour one third of the chocolate mixture into the base of the liner. Transfer to the refrigerator and leave for 20–30 minutes, until just set.

4 Shape the peanut butter mixture into an 18-cm/7-inch round and gently place it on top of the set chocolate.

5 If necessary, re-melt the remaining chocolate. Pour over the peanut butter filling to cover it completely, then gently level the surface. Chill in the refrigerator until set.

6 To serve, remove the peanut butter cup from the paper lining. Place on a flat serving plate and leave to stand at room temperature for about 1 hour, then slice into wedges with a sharp knife.

CHURROS

Makes: 16

Prep: 30 mins, plus cooling

Cook: 25–30 mins

Ingredients

- 225 ml/8 fl oz water
- 85 g/3 oz butter or lard, diced
- 2 tbsp dark muscovado sugar
- finely grated rind of 1 small orange (optional)
- pinch of salt
- 175 g/6 oz plain flour, sifted
- 1 tsp ground cinnamon, plus extra for dusting
- 1 tsp vanilla extract
- 2 eggs
- oil, for deep-frying
- caster sugar, for dusting

Method

1. Heat the water, butter, muscovado sugar, orange rind, if using, and salt in a heavy-based saucepan over a medium heat until the butter has melted. Add the flour, all at once, the cinnamon and vanilla extract, then remove the saucepan from the heat and beat rapidly until the mixture pulls away from the side of the saucepan.
2. Leave to cool slightly, then beat in the eggs, one at a time, beating well after each addition, until the mixture is thick and smooth. Spoon into a piping bag fitted with a wide star nozzle.
3. Heat enough oil for deep-frying in a large saucepan or deep-fryer to 180–190°C/350–375°F, or until a cube of bread browns in 30 seconds. Pipe 13-cm/5-inch lengths about 7.5 cm/3 inches apart into the hot oil. Fry for 2–3 minutes, turning frequently, until crisp and golden. Remove with a slotted spoon and drain on kitchen paper. Keep warm while frying the remaining mixture.
4. Dust with caster sugar and cinnamon to serve.

★ Variation

To make a chocolate dipping sauce, melt 85 g/3 oz plain chocolate with 100 ml/3½ fl oz double cream, then stir in ½ teaspoon vanilla extract.

1
3

DRY MARTINI

Serves: 1 **Prep: 10 mins** **Cook: N/A**

Ingredients

4–6 cracked ice cubes
1 measure London dry gin
dash dry vermouth
cocktail olive, to decorate

Method

1 Put the cracked ice into a cocktail shaker. Pour over the gin and vermouth.
2 Shake until well frosted.
3 Strain into a chilled glass and decorate with the olive. Serve immediately.

2
3

MARGARITA

Serves: 1 **Prep: 10–12 mins** **Cook: N/A**

Ingredients

2 lime slices
coarse salt
4–6 cracked ice cubes
3 measures white tequila
1 measure Triple Sec or Cointreau
2 measures lime juice

Method

1 Rub the rim of a chilled cocktail glass with a lime slice. Dip in a saucer of coarse salt.

2 Put the cracked ice cubes into a cocktail shaker. Pour over the tequila, Triple Sec and lime juice and shake vigorously until well frosted. Strain into the glass.

3 Decorate with the remaining lime slice. Serve immediately.

2
3

FROZEN STRAWBERRY DAIQUIRIS

Serves: 2

Prep: 12–15 mins, plus cooling

Cook: 5 mins

Ingredients

400 g/14 oz strawberries
8 ice cubes
100 ml/3½ fl oz white rum
50 ml/2 fl oz lime juice

Sugar syrup

55 g/2 oz caster sugar
75 ml/2½ fl oz water

Method

1 To make the sugar syrup, put the sugar and water in a saucepan and heat gently, stirring until the sugar has dissolved. Bring to the boil, then cook, without stirring, over a medium heat for 2 minutes. Remove from the heat and leave to cool slightly.

2 Hull and slice the strawberries, leaving two whole for decoration.

3 Crush the ice in a blender. Add two teaspoons of the cooled sugar syrup to the ice (you can store the remaining sugar syrup in the refrigerator for several weeks).

4 Add the rum, lime juice and sliced strawberries. Blend until slushy, then pour into chilled cocktail glasses. Decorate the side of the glasses with whole strawberries.

3
4

CLUB MOJITO

Serves: 1 **Prep: 10 mins** **Cook: N/A**

Ingredients

1 tsp sugar syrup
6 fresh mint leaves
juice of ½ lime
4–6 cracked ice cubes
2 measures Jamaican rum
soda water
dash Angostura bitters

Method

1 Put the sugar syrup, mint leaves and lime juice into a chilled glass.

2 Muddle the mint leaves, then add the cracked ice cubes and the rum.

3 Top up with soda water and finish with the Angostura bitters. Serve immediately.

COSMOPOLITAN

Serves: 1 **Prep: 10 mins** **Cook: N/A**

Ingredients

4–6 cracked ice cubes
2 measures vodka
1 measure Triple Sec
1 measure lime juice
1 measure cranberry juice
strip of orange zest, to decorate

Method

1 Put the cracked ice cubes into a cocktail shaker.

2 Pour the liquid ingredients over the ice cubes. Shake vigorously until well frosted.

3 Strain into a chilled cocktail glass and decorate with the orange zest.

1
2
3

TEQUILA SLAMMER

Serves: 1 **Prep: 10 mins** **Cook: N/A**

Ingredients

1 measure silver tequila, chilled

juice of ½ lemon

sparkling wine, chilled

Method

1 Put the tequila into a chilled shot glass. Add the lemon juice.

2 Top up with sparkling wine.

3 Cover the glass with your hand and slam to mix. Serve immediately.

SANGRIA

Serves: 6

Prep: 15–20 mins, plus marinating

Cook: N/A

Ingredients

juice of 1 orange
juice of 1 lemon
2 tbsp icing sugar
cracked ice
1 orange, thinly sliced
1 lemon, thinly sliced
1 bottle chilled red wine
lemonade, to taste

Method

1 Put the orange juice and lemon juice in a large jug.

2 Add the sugar and stir. When the sugar has dissolved, add 4–6 cracked ice cubes.

3 Add the sliced fruit and the wine and leave to marinate for 1 hour.

4 Add lemonade to taste, then top up with cracked ice. Serve immediately.

BLOODY MARY

Serves: 6 **Prep: 10–15 mins** **Cook: N/A**

Ingredients

4–6 cracked ice cubes
dash hot pepper sauce
dash Worcestershire sauce
2 measures vodka
6 measures tomato juice
juice of ½ lemon
pinch celery salt
pinch cayenne pepper
celery stick and lemon slice, to decorate

Method

1 Put the cracked ice cubes into a cocktail shaker. Dash the hot pepper sauce and Worcestershire sauce over the ice.

2 Add the vodka and tomato juice. Squeeze in the juice from the lemon half and shake vigorously until well frosted.

3 Strain into a chilled highball glass. Add the celery salt and cayenne pepper and decorate with the celery stick and lemon slice. Serve immediately.

1
2
2

SHIRLEY TEMPLE

Serves: 1 **Prep: 10 mins** **Cook: N/A**

Ingredients

cracked ice cubes
2 measures lemon juice
½ measure grenadine
½ measure sugar syrup
ginger ale
orange slice, to decorate

Method

1 Put 4–6 cracked ice cubes into a cocktail shaker.
2 Pour over the lemon juice, grenadine and sugar syrup and shake vigorously until well frosted.
3 Half-fill a chilled highball glass with cracked ice, then strain the cocktail over it.
4 Top up with ginger ale and decorate with the orange slice. Serve immediately.

1
2
3

RASPBERRY LEMONADE

Serves: 4 **Prep: 15 mins** **Cook: N/A**

Ingredients

2 lemons
115 g/4 oz icing sugar
115 g/4 oz raspberries
few drops vanilla extract
cracked ice cubes
sparkling water
fresh mint sprigs, to decorate

Method

1 Cut the ends off the lemons, then scoop out and chop the flesh.

2 Put the lemon flesh in a blender with the sugar, raspberries, vanilla extract and 4–6 cracked ice cubes. Blend for 2–3 minutes.

3 Half-fill four chilled highball glasses with cracked ice and strain in the lemon and raspberry mixture.

4 Top up with sparkling water and decorate with mint sprigs. Serve immediately.

★ Variation

For a classic lemonade, put 150 ml/5 fl oz water, 6 tablespoons sugar and 1 teaspoon grated lemon rind in a small saucepan and bring to the boil, stirring constantly. Continue to boil, stirring, for 5 minutes. Remove from the heat and leave to cool. Stir in 125 ml/4 fl oz lemon juice, then chill for at least 2 hours. Fill two glasses with cracked ice, pour in the chilled lemon syrup and top up with sparkling water.

INDEX

This edition published by Parragon Books Ltd in 2016
LOVE FOOD is an imprint of Parragon Books Ltd

Parragon Books Ltd
Chartist House
15–17 Trim Street
Bath BA1 1HA, UK

www.parragon.com/lovefood

ISBN 978-1-4723-6462-3
Printed in China

Introduction by Anne Sheasby

Notes for the Reader
This book uses both metric and imperial measurements. Follow the same units of measurement throughout; do not mix metric and imperial. All spoon measurements are level: teaspoons are assumed to be 5 ml, and tablespoons are assumed to be 15 ml. Unless otherwise stated, milk is assumed to be full fat, eggs and individual vegetables are medium, and pepper is freshly ground black pepper. Unless otherwise stated, all root vegetables should be peeled prior to using.

Garnishes, decorations and serving suggestions are all optional and not necessarily included in the recipe ingredients or method. The times given are an approximate guide only. Preparation times differ according to the techniques used by different people and the cooking times may also vary from those given. Optional ingredients, variations or serving suggestions have not been included in the time calculations.